WINNERS
ARE DRIVEN

WINNERS
ARE DRIVEN

A CHAMPION'S GUIDE TO SUCCESS
IN BUSINESS & LIFE

BOBBY UNSER

WITH PAUL PEASE

WILEY

John Wiley & Sons, Inc.

Published by John Wiley & Sons, Inc., Hoboken, New Jersey.
Published simultaneously in Canada.

For general information on our other products and services, or technical support, please
contact our Customer Care Department within the United States at 800-762-2974, outside
the United States at 317-572-3993 or fax 317-572-4002.

Wiley also publishes its books in a variety of electronic formats. Some content that appears
in print may not be available in electronic books.

For more information about Wiley products, visit our web site at www.wiley.com.

Library of Congress Cataloging-in-Publication Data:

Unser, Bobby.
    Winners are driven : a champion's guide to success in business and
  life / Bobby Unser with Paul Pease.
        p.   cm.
    Includes index.
    ISBN 0-471-25068-6 (CLOTH : alk. paper)
    1. Success in business.   2. Success.   I. Pease, Paul.   II. Title.
  HF5386 .U515 2003
  650.1—dc21

                                                            2002014046

Printed in the United States of America
10 9 8 7 6 5 4 3 2 1

*Nobody remembers who finished second
but the guy who finished second.*

CONTENTS

FOREWORD

We've had many great racecar drivers on Team Penske: Mark Donohue, Al Unser, Sr., Tom Sneva, Rick Mears, Mario Andretti, Emerson Fittipaldi, Al Unser, Jr., Danny Sullivan, Gil de Ferran, and Helio Castroneves, to name just a few. Bobby Unser ranks among our most prolific winners of all time. He won 11 of 37 races—almost one out of every three races—in the three years he drove for Team Penske and in that time he helped develop four different Penske cars.

I had watched Bobby as a competitor; he was bright, worked extremely hard and always endeavored to get the most out of his equipment. He understood the intricacies of each car and figured out what might coax an extra mile or two per hour from it. Bobby's success on the track was fueled by his desire to constantly improve more than any other driver on the circuit.

What gave him an edge over the others was his early background in racing. He didn't start out as just a driver, but also as a mechanic, and after that, he built his own cars. Later he focused on driving, but it was this early upbringing in the business—knowing the inner workings of the whole racing operation from the bottom up—that was an integral part of Bobby's winning arsenal.

In 1978, Team Penske not only needed a new top driver, but a driver with the ability to help the team test and further develop our Penske-built cars. When Bobby was with us, we would engineer the car, then give it to him to find more speed and better performance. That's how learning from the ground up proved helpful: Bobby's vast experience as a mechanic and his natural engineering talent had honed his sixth sense for racing. These factors allowed him to make quick decisions as a driver in order to get more speed out of the car.

Bobby's intelligence, aggressiveness, and determination blended together, resulting in a powerfully competitive race driver. Even more amazing, he accomplished his great numbers with Team Penske between the ages of 45 and 47—past retirement age for most drivers. By the time he raced for us, Bobby had already competed in over 4000 races, yet he still approached every race as though it were his first. He never showed signs of slowing down.

Though it's been nearly a quarter of a century since he drove for Team Penske, Bobby Unser still hasn't slowed down.

ACKNOWLEDGMENTS

There are so many people who helped me along the way that I need to thank—so many that I'm sure I'll miss a few. The most supportive and influential people include:

My family: Daddy, Jerry Unser Sr. and Mom, Mary Craven Unser; Uncle Louis Unser; Jerry Unser Jr., Louis Unser, and Al Unser (my brothers). Without them, there would be no Bobby Unser success story to write. Bruce Barnes my agent and business partner for over thirty years who helped put this book project together deserves special mention. He has done so many good things for me and my career. My wife Lisa has done a tremendous amount of work helping reconstruct over forty years of racing history through my numerous photo albums and newspaper clippings.

Other people who helped as well during my career, some of whom are mentioned in the book, include Dennis Swanson, the President of ABC when I was a color commentator for ABC, and my biggest supporters in racing, the people of the Goodyear Tire and Rubber Company: Leo Mehl, Ed Alexander, and Vic Holt.

And there were the many great racecar owners I drove for: Bob Wilke, Andy Granatelli, Roger Penske, Dan Gurney, Smokey Yunick, Parnelli Jones, Jack Zink, Frank Arciero, Don Sheppard, Bud Trainor, George Tallant, Gordon Van Liew, and all the sprint car and midget car owners I drove for over many years.

Others who helped me succeed in my career were Ralph Moody (Ford Stock cars) and Bunky Knudson (President of Ford). A special thank-you to Jo Hoppen of Audi, where we set 16 world records at Talladega, and then won Pikes Peak in 1986 with a new record.

I devoted a whole chapter to people who helped, but I'll mention a few names here: People who helped build, set up, and maintain the racecars, like Wayne Leary, John Miller, and each of Dan Gurney's All American Racers, people who built the fabulous Eagle Race Cars: then, from Team Penske, Jerry Breon, Laurie Garrish, Clive Howell, Nick Goozee, Jeff Ferris, Carl Keinhauffer, and the rest of the crew at Penske's facility in England: from my early big wins in Indy cars, Jud Phillips, Tom "Little Red" Herrmann, and the Leader Card racing crew. Finally, I can't forget my good friend, Howard Millican, who was my mechanic and crew on many Pikes Peak Hill Climbs and Sports Car races.

Thanks also go to the people who helped put this book together: Howard Cohl of Mi-5, Paul Pease, Nancy Ellis, and Deb Englander and the people of John Wiley and Sons; Donald Davidson of the Indianapolis Motor Speedway Museum and Dick Jordan of USAC who provided some great background and statistical information; and the Indianapolis Motor Speedway that provided great photos. All of these people, I thank sincerely for helping put the book together. All the people who helped with my career, I thank you for providing me the life-lessons in these pages.

INTRODUCTION

I've spent the better part of my teenage and adult life racing cars for a living, driving in over 4000 races. But I never thought that all I ever was supposed to do was drive racecars. Racing to me was much more than being a driver. It was about desire, passion, failure, education, wins, trust, teamwork, and the fans. All these aspects of racing helped me become successful in business.

I never really retired from racing: I just retired from *what* I was racing. It's no longer cars—now it's business. The lessons I learned to be a successful racecar driver helped me be a successful businessman. I view my entire adult life as having been a businessman. To me, there is no better metaphor for business than racing. All the attributes of what it takes to succeed in life can be found at every race track. It doesn't matter if what's being run on those tracks are Indy cars, sprint cars, dragsters, or stock cars.

If you look carefully at auto racing, you'll find incredible desire by everyone associated with a team, especially the driver, who literally puts his life on the line. You'll find incredible teamwork in a pit stop. You'll find unselfish behavior in which the good of the many outweighs the needs of the individual. Race teams have indomitable leadership by team owners and crew chiefs who know how to manage and motivate others, and an unquestionable belief by the teammates themselves that the leaders can guide them to victory. Well-run race teams function like a business, and well-run businesses operate like race teams.

And you'll find a most incredible dynamic in the relationship between the race teams, sponsors, and the fans. Like a Wal-Mart executive
doing store checks to gauge consumer attitudes, race fans, sponsors, and
race teams commingle in paddock areas at every track. Race teams and
sponsors *always* know what fans are thinking!

In my years of interacting with companies of all sizes, public and private—as an owner, consultant, spokesperson, or customer—I've found
that my experience in racing has made me a better businessman. As a
principal in many ventures ranging from automobile dealerships to
marketing service companies to real estate investment groups, I've become much more knowledgeable about what it *really* takes to succeed
because of racing and the fabulous mentors who guided me. Men like
Dennis Swanson and Roger Penske, and countless others who passed
along their wisdom openly and freely. Not always without a raised
voice, but always with the best interests in mind.

The lessons I learned about business through my successes and failures in racing (and I've had a lot of failures!) can help you on your path
to winning in whatever race you chose to run. I think you'll find that
each of the strategies I discuss will have some application to your professional lives. It may not occur immediately, but I suspect that at some
point down the road you'll be in a situation and you'll say to yourself,
"So that's what Bobby Unser meant." When that happens, please drop
me a note at BobbyUnser@aol.com, as I'd love to hear about it.

I hope the ride you're about to take with me is as enjoyable for you as
it was for me.

CHAPTER ONE

FIRE IN THE BELLY

*L*ap number 170, time for what I hope is the last pit stop of the race. I bust out of turn four at 200 miles per hour, and pull the Eagle-Offy out down into pit row. Every second off the track is costing us 100 yards in the race, so I have to stay at full speed as long as I can before slowing down. As I approach my pit area, I start to downshift and brake hard, really hard. Now for the most strenuous and stressful part of the race: Changing tires and adding fuel in 12 seconds, while I keep the engine running.

I pull over to my pit area and stop. My right heel keeps the throttle pushed in so the engine is still turning 6000 rpm. The ball of my right foot holds the brake in, and my left foot is holding the narrow one and one-half inch wide by three-inch long clutch pedal in.

1 second . . .

The vent man plugs in the air hose and the car pops up. I relax my cramped, bleeding fingers from their steel grip on the steering wheel for the first time in 33 laps. Man, that was about 30 minutes ago. The leather gloves have worn through, and somehow a few new blisters have grown between the calluses. The only leather that isn't worn out now is the piece of gum I've been chewing for the last three plus hours—my jaw is sore, but at least my throat isn't dry. I'm sweating like a pig in the Indianapolis heat, and the damn Gatorade sitting next to the radiator is hotter than hot tea. I don't drink hot tea on a hot day.

Two, three, four seconds . . .

As the tires are changed and the Offy guzzles its fuel, I move my fatigued shoulders to loosen the tension that comes from being stuck in one position for over three hours. They have been locked into position since I folded my-self into my car seat at the start of the race. My seat doesn't allow me to move; it's made out of leather and a fiberglass mold that is shaped to my body. This is Bobby Unser's seat—nobody else can fit in this thing. It's a molded straitjacket. Once I'm in, I'm not going to move.

My muscles really get strained being pulled by two and half to three Gs every time I go through a turn. I'm 165 pounds, and when I pull three Gs through a turn, I'm adding three times the force of gravity to my body. I'm essentially getting a 495-pound person to sit on me through that turn as I try to control the car and keep it off the wall coming into the straight. If I run my lines through turn three into the back straight, I'll pull out at over 200 miles per hour twelve inches from the wall. Every turn of the race is a new adventure as the race progresses—debris, oil, wind speed and direction, and cars are constantly changing. After 170 laps, I've done 680 turns— sometimes one every twelve seconds, and each one totally different than the other.

Between my prerace nerves, the Indianapolis sun, the heat, and the noise, the only thing that is keeping the pain from exploding my head is my hel-met. I peel off my second of three visor sheets—coated with sand and oil, leaving me one tear-off sheet just in case I need it near the end of the race.

Five, six seconds . . .

I move my almost-numb legs for one last time. I've had to pee since the start of the race. I was so excited before the race, I forgot to pee. That hap-pens when you have to perform before the largest single sporting event in the world against the thirty-two most conditioned athletes in the world— 400,000 people in the stands and millions more watching on television. The stakes don't get any higher, the stage doesn't get any bigger. The Indy 500 is the biggest professional sports spectator event in the world. Period.

Seven, eight seconds . . .

The tires are done. I grip the wheel for one last stretch run. The vent man pops the air hose and I feel the car drop back down to the ground. I push *my right heel in to rev the engine up to 9000 rpm, lighting the turbocharger, and 1000 horsepower roars to life.*

Nine seconds, ten seconds . . .

My fuel man is the key to this whole pit stop—his job takes the longest, and as soon as he's done, I know I can go. I'm watching him in my peripheral vision beside me to my left. Simultaneously, I'm watching my right front man, Wayne Leary, because he will give me the wave when it's clear to go.

Eleven, twelve seconds . . .

I know Wayne so well, I don't have to wait for him to give me the signal to go—I can see it in his eyes. His eyes light up, let's go! I leave as fast as I can without tearing the car up—I can't break the transmission or the rear axle. The clutch is out and I haul ass out of the pits. Thirty laps to go— seventy-five miles and twenty-plus minutes of 200 mile per hour blood, sweat, and holding my breath.

There's no room for error now. I don't dare make a mistake so close to the end and a possible win. There's a couple of hundred thousand dollars at stake now—sponsors, family, and over 100 million TV fans are watching this exciting finish to the greatest spectacle on earth. God, I love this job!

You can't start or finish a race without fuel in the tank. In your quest for success, that fuel is desire. Managers, coaches, athletes, and career consultants are often asked why some people succeed and others do not. There are many ingredients to success, but without a question, in my opinion, desire is the most important. Desire allows us to overcome obstacles on our quest to reach our goals. Obstacles include competitors, financial issues, weather, and our own fears. For example, I have a fear of heights. I'm a pilot and have my own plane, and I'm scared to death to climb a ladder. I've won Pikes Peak a record 13 times, yet I'm afraid to look over the edge. Desire drives us past our obstacles that hold us back from succeeding.

Successful racecar drivers always get asked by fans, "What should I do to become a successful driver like you?" I tell everyone the same thing: If you want to become a great driver, get in a car and figure out how to make it go faster. You don't have to search for a magic formula because there is none. But, you must first have desire. This applies not only to racing, but to any endeavor in which you wish to be successful. Desire comes from the soul, and it is what makes the good become great and turns the great into legends.

WHY DESIRE IS SO IMPORTANT

There are many "naturally" talented drivers in racing—gifted people who were born with the physical build and stamina as well as great reactive instincts. Hence, it comes "natural" to them. Suppose you were to take this naturally talented person and put him or her in a race with a person who is not as naturally talented, but who has much more desire. Who do you think has the better odds of winning? What would happen if you took someone and gave him or her the best car and had that individual race against the person with the most desire, but in not as good a car? Who would most likely win?

Desire gives you the ability to overcome obstacles, such as equipment failures and bad weather. When you have desire, you don't blame the equipment or circumstances for your failings. You deal with the situation and put things back together, get back up, and charge forward again. With desire you do not depend on external factors, such as good weather or good equipment, to achieve your goals. You can perform independent of the externals, so even if they fail, they don't control you or your destiny. Desire gives you internal control. It is *your* engine that provides the power to run the race.

Desire may not beat superior equipment or the more talented the first time around. It may not win the second time around. But in time, the people with desire will always rise to the top. They don't quit. They don't take anything for granted. They don't let obstacles stop them. If you were dealt four cards in a card game and they were desire, talent, money, and equipment, desire eventually trumps the other three.

Frank Arciero is an example of the power of desire. Frank is a good friend and was one of my early racing owners. He gave many good drivers the opportunity to race. Dan Gurney, Al (my brother), and myself are indebted to Frank and his belief in us as highly competitive drivers.

Frank is also a fabulous businessman. He came to the United States from Italy in the early 1950s. Frank had no formal education in how to run a business and he was new to the country, culture, and language. But those factors didn't prevent Frank from becoming extremely successful. He wanted something more, and he saw that working in the United States provided an opportunity to meet that goal.

Frank's first job was digging ditches for a construction company. By proving himself and working hard, he was promoted to crew supervisor. With this promotion, Frank used his personal skills and teamwork concepts to lay the groundwork to move to the next level of construction site foreman. Propelling himself through his desire to do more—learning management skills and project costs—he became a construction project manager. Eventually, Frank became a full-fledged contractor, owning and running his own construction firm. As an immigrant and without any formal education, it took a long time for Frank Arciero to make it to the top. His desire is what made it happen.

WHAT IGNITES DESIRE?

I consider myself to be a student of desire. I love to figure out what motivates people. In a race, it's imperative to know what makes a driver tick. I want to know how he is going to react under different circumstances during a race. In my 40 years of studying desire, I've come to the conclusion that there are five general sources of this elusive attribute:

1. Desire by inspiration
2. Desire by deprivation
3. Desire by integrity
4. Desire by competition
5. Desire by respect

Desire by Inspiration

Without question, inspirational people instill desire in individuals. We look up to these inspirational individuals. Personally, my daddy was someone I admired. He was an entrepreneur, always trying things, always innovating. He failed and failed and failed until he became successful through continuous hard work and perseverance.

Daddy started out in the auto repair business near Colorado Springs during the Great Depression in the early 1930s. He had the Ute Pass Garage in Manitou, Colorado, on the road to Pikes Peak. Colorado Springs was a tourist town, and after Labor Day, tourism died. It picked up again in June after Memorial Day. During the Depression, without any money, he had to hunt and fish for our food. Life boiled down to the basics: Do everything you could each day to provide food, clothing, and shelter for the family. With Mom and three little boys, there were some hungry mouths to feed.

During the Depression years, finding work was impossible—there just weren't any jobs. So Daddy started his own business. But, the Ute Pass Garage didn't make it financially and he closed it. He tried another auto repair business in Colorado Springs. That didn't work either. Then he opened a restaurant. After the restaurant failed, he packed up everything and moved the family to Albuquerque, New Mexico. We were so poor that he had to sell our car to finance the move to Albuquerque by train.

After arriving in Albuquerque, Daddy went to work in a salvage yard. He always wanted to own and run his own business, but he also had to provide for the family. He saved every penny he could while still feeding, clothing, and housing us. After he saved enough money, he bought some land west of Albuquerque on Highway 66, and built an auto repair garage with a few gas pumps and a house. He built it entirely by himself by doing the plumbing, electric, and everything else. When you don't have the financial resources to pay for things, you do them yourself; that's how entrepreneurs become successful. They make something out of nothing by the sheer desire to get something done.

The Highway 66 garage really started to do well until December 7, 1941. When Pearl Harbor was bombed and the United States entered World War II, everything changed. Daddy wanted to serve the country, but the military wouldn't take him. By then Al was born, and now Daddy had four boys to feed. Daddy was a decorated World War I Navy veteran, but the Navy didn't want to take a dad with four sons.

So instead, he volunteered to help the Army build Camp Hale in the mountains of Colorado. He understood priorities, and his country was a priority over his business. The garage and house on Highway 66 were completely boarded up, our belongings boxed up, the family—Mom, Daddy, the four boys, and Rita, who Daddy had hired in Albuquerque to care for us while he and Mom worked at his business, and who he didn't want to leave out in the cold with no job—all crammed into our car and moved to Leadville, Colorado. There were no places to live in Leadville, so we had to move to a cabin on the lake 35 miles to the west. The cabin was built in the 1800s. There was no electricity, no running water, and no indoor plumbing. We had a Coleman lantern for light, an outhouse for a toilet, and we retrieved water from the lake. Jerry and Louis were seven years old, I was six, and Al was only two. We had to learn to fish to eat. Daddy only came home once a week, and on a good weekend he would bring home one quart of milk that was shared among the four boys. One block of ice would help keep the milk fresh for the week. Eventually, we moved to a nicer house in Buena Vista.

Buena Vista was a long commute for Daddy, but it was a much better place for us to live. We would swim in the Arkansas River and fish, and we would catch frogs, roast their legs, and eat them for lunch. We became little mountain boys: We were fed breakfast, went out to find our frogs, then had lunch and went home.

After Daddy finished building Camp Hale in 1944, we moved back to Albuquerque. He opened up the house and garage, and he was back in business. Even though we were situated on Highway 66, the main thoroughfare from the East to the West Coast, business was still tough. With World War II in full swing, everything including gasoline and rubber was rationed. That really reduced the traffic on Highway 66 and forced Daddy to get creative.

With the rationing, there weren't many tourists, but there were a lot of GIs passing through to the East and West Coasts. Even the GIs had gas and tires rationed to them. For gasoline, the government figured out what their gas mileage was, and how far they were going. Then they gave them a certain allotment of stamps to get them to where they were going, and that was it. If their cars didn't get the mileage the government thought they should get, they didn't make it to their destinations.

Tires were just as bad. If they had a blowout, which was common, they had to fix it or leave the car because they weren't going to get another tire.

Since the rationing was so restrictive, by the time some of the GIs got to Albuquerque, they realized they weren't going to make it to their destinations. Either they didn't have enough gas stamps to make it, or their tires were junk. In some cases, they had both issues to deal with.

Daddy would do everything he could to help these GIs get to their destination and keep their cars. He would figure out how to get them more stamps so they could get gas. Technically, this was illegal, but Daddy never did anything illegal to help himself financially. He was doing it to help the GIs. The alternative with no more gas was to leave their cars and take the train. The GIs had to get to their destinations, and they needed their cars when they got there. So daddy did everything he could to help the GI's get to California—or wherever they were going—and keep their cars.

Daddy also tuned up their cars to get better gas mileage. He'd clean the filters, pumps, and adjust the mixture on the carburetors—anything to get another mile or two per gallon on their cars. Every mile per gallon was another 20 miles closer to California per fill-up for the GIs. These creative innovations were later applied to our racing endeavors.

Daddy would often make custom wheels for a car to fit the tires. For example, if the customer had a 16-inch wheel, but he could only get 15-inch tires, he would make a 15-inch wheel for the GI, and customize it to the GI's car. He would even go to the junkyard, get two wheels, cut them in half, and re-weld them together to make one wheel.

Not all the people who had garages on Highway 66 were as upstanding and helpful as my daddy. Bud Rice had a place on Highway 66 about 60 miles west of Albuquerque in Budville, New Mexico. He'd do things to break the cars, and then financially break the GIs. He was a bad person who gave auto repair a bad name. Someone eventually shot and killed him. He reaped what he sowed.

Look at business people you respect. Think about why you respect them. More than likely it is because they have the desire to do what they do. They enjoy what they do, and continuously work at perfecting their craft. Sometimes they succeed, sometimes they fail, but no matter what happens, they have the desire to continue the journey.

In the racing business, the consistently successful teams are the ones that are led by example. Parnelli Jones, Roger Penske, Dan Gurney, Bob Wilke—even some of my sprint car owners such as Don Shepherd—are legendary when it comes to showing desire by example. They consistently had good teams, which can be attributed to showing desire in everything they did. They set the pace for their people to follow. Parnelli had the fire in his eyes as a driver, and you could see that intensity when he raced. Roger Penske showed his passion for the racing business by how he thought a situation through and then moved decisively. He also knew how to help his people succeed by giving them the tools and his leadership support to help them accomplish their goals. Dan Gurney was an absolute genius when it came to engineering racing breakthroughs. Bob Wilke's people-sense helped him bring in the right people for his racing teams. All of these people were highly successful in racing, each in his own way. The common bond was their passion—their desire—to succeed.

Vic Holt of Goodyear, Harold Hollnagel of Mechanical Industries, and Ben Bendixen of Robert Bosch Corporation were not only good racing sponsors, but great leaders of their companies. Vic Holt was like Bob Wilke—he knew how to recruit good people. Leo Mehl, Ed Alexander, and Larry Trusdale were all gold-plated people working with Vic Holt. Harold Hollnagel owns one of the few companies—Mechanical Industries—that actively helps its employees succeed in their careers. Mechanical Industries provides employee trade and career training and educational development programs, and also partners with local trade and continuing education programs in the Milwaukee area. Ben Bendixen has a passion—a fire—for providing quality solutions to the automotive market. Just as the successful people in the racing business have various ways to succeed in racing, so too are these leaders bonded by one common thread: desire. Any great leader shows the path by lighting it with desire. New leaders use their examples as a way to light new paths to success.

When you think about whether or not you have the desire to accomplish your goal, think about the people you admire. Think about what it is you admire in them. You'll realize it's not necessarily their wealth that you admire, but instead it is the journey they took—the

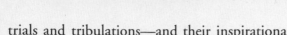

trials and tribulations—and their inspirational approach to business. Find good examples of desire and follow them. Then use your own desire to set the example for others to follow.

Desire by Deprivation

Don't you love to pull for the underdog? People like to cheer for the underdog, which is a good reason why small businesses are often successful when competing against those that are much larger. Small-business owners figure out how to do more with less, and win despite the odds. They don't have all of the resources to win, but instead find a way to utilize the resources they have to their best advantage.

Our family used deprivation to get creative when it came to racing at Pikes Peak. The Pikes Peak Hill Climb is the second oldest race in the United States, starting in 1916. The race has remained basically the same throughout history. It is run one car at a time, with set starting intervals between each car. The race starts at 9500 feet and finishes 12.5 miles later, at 14,110 feet after 160 treacherous edge-of-the cliff turns, at the summit. The Hill Climb is run on a pulverized granite road, which can be dusty, muddy, and icy during the same race. There can be rain, hail, sleet, snow, wind, and sun during any given race. It's a very challenging race, but also a lot of fun to drive.

Daddy and his brothers, Louis and Joe, rode motorcycles up to the top of Pikes Peak in 1915, a year before the first race between motorcycles and cars. Jerry, Louis (my older twin brothers), and I started racing at Pikes Peak in 1955. Unsers had been racing to the top of Pikes Peak for over 40 years by the time my brothers and I raced there.

Unfortunately, we were woefully short on resources, mainly money. Tires become critical in that case, but we couldn't afford the racing tires that Firestone made especially for the Hill Climb. We were boxed in with our lack of money, so we had to be creative. To make up for our inability to afford new tires, we bought used tires and recapped them. These tires ended up being better for racing Pikes Peak than the new Firestones.

We recapped tires at a place in Colorado Springs that could do it in one day, thus cutting the development time. We impregnated the tires with ground-up battery casings and tried walnut shells of different sizes.

The combination of walnut shells and batteries would make the tire act like a sponge and grip the road better. We discovered the walnut shells performed better than the ground-up batteries. Our desire to race did not prohibit us from racing, despite our financial limitations. We found a way to race, and it turned out to be a far better way.

Deprivation isn't a tactic; it's truly deprivation. You don't get desire by falsely depriving yourself of resources to force creativity. There must be a balance between the two extremes. Somewhere between throwing money at a problem and starving yourself to death you hit a balance point that keeps your creative juices flowing. You have to stay a little hungry to win.

I recently read an article about Scott McNealy of Sun Microsystems, and he and his top people seem to understand this concept thoroughly. Scott is quoted in a conversation with *Business Week* editor-in-chief Stephen B. Shepard, April 1, 2002, "A Talk With Scott McNealy":

> *(Sun Chief Scientist) Bill Joy likes to say there's never been a success-ful well-funded startup. If you have too much money, you're not going to find a new and different and more efficient and more effective way. You're just going to try and overpower the current players with the same strategy.*

Desire by Integrity

Have you ever had someone box you in with an unfair interpretation of a rule, change the rules as the game is being played, or do something that intentionally made things difficult for you to perform your job? It happens often, and it's another fuel source for desire. You want to fix things, but the right way. This is not revenge, although revenge seems to be the motive. This is genuinely righting a wrong. Typically the wrong is done when someone prohibits you from achieving a goal by creating or changing the playing rules.

When we were using recapped tires for Pikes Peak, we started to win a lot of races. This caused a problem for the Hill Climb Officials. One of their big sponsors was the Firestone Tire and Rubber Company. We couldn't afford the Firestone tires, but now were winning on non-Firestones at a Firestone-sponsored event. That's not good advertising for Firestone. The problem was that instead of being competitive by developing a tire that could beat us, they took the easy way out: eliminate the Unsers from the Hill Climb. The excuse they used was that our recapped tires were "unsafe."

This often happens in business when someone wants to stack the deck in favor of a pet person or project, even though there's supposed to be an open opportunity. They just want the good old boys to stay intact. They don't like change because change threatens them. If you have the desire to make changes, use this challenge of beating the good old boys network as a means to fuel your desire to right the wrong by winning anyway.

As it turns out, we fought the Hill Climb Officials on the tire rule change. Daddy got a court injunction to halt the race until the ruling could be reviewed by a judge. Just prior to the scheduled race date, he dropped the injunction. He really didn't want the race to be stopped. We weren't too happy about this whole mess, and begrudgingly raced on the Firestone tires they ended up giving us. We won the race anyway. Then we started to work with Goodyear to develop a new racing tire for the following year's race. Righting a wrong fueled a desire that not only proved our point of doing right, but also pushed us to get Goodyear into the automobile racing business, investing millions of dollars. Goodyear would wind up investing up to $20 million per year in racing tire development.

Desire by Competition

Another fuel additive for desire is the competitive spirit. It's not so much the need to win as it is the need not to lose. All the Unser boys—the eldest being twins, Jerry and Louis, then me, and the youngest, Al—were very competitive. We used to compete with each other for everything. Catching rattlesnakes, shooting a .22 caliber gun, or racing donkeys—we competed in everything we did. When we'd catch rattlesnakes, it was who could catch the most rattlesnakes, or the biggest. Mind you, we didn't compete stupidly, like who could get bit the most. It was always who could catch the most without getting bit. Daddy gave us a .22 single-shot rifle. After watching a movie that showed a cowboy lighting matches with his gun, we had to compete to see who could do that the best. We'd stick a dozen wooden matches in the ground and see who could light the most. This was probably where I learned to be a good marksman, because in order to light the match, you had to have the bullet graze the very tip of the match without hitting it. We had donkeys we'd race. That's probably where we learned to strategize for racing, because if you picked a fast donkey, you also picked one that bucked the most. So the risk was speed over getting tossed. If you picked a more tame one, you'd finish the race, but might lose to the fastest one if the rider wasn't bucked. Everything was competitive among the Unsers, but in a good way that helped us years later in our racing careers. At first, we had to share the Pontiac Daddy gave us one Christmas, but we all had our own way to drive, our own desires. As soon as we were able to, we got our own cars and competed with each other. There's no way I would let my brother Al beat me. We were nice to each other off the track, but when that green flag dropped, I always tried my hardest to not let him beat me.

There are certain competitors who bring out the fires of performance in all of us. Mario Andretti is a competitor I really like off the track, but when that race started—it was all-out war. We need this competitive edge fueling our desire because there are always too many people trying to be first.

The competitive edge provides the adrenaline boost to overcome your opponent. It's like having another gear to shift to when you need it. You get this by really pushing at a given moment, or by learning the opponent's tendencies and defeating him that way. Rick Mears was known as a driver who would hold back for 150 of the 200 laps in the Indy 500. Then he would come on strong and pour it on at the finish. He'd reserve himself for the last fourth of the race.

We always knew Rick would make his move somewhere around lap 150. The pit crew would radio to me when he was starting to make his move. I'd watch for him in the rearview mirror until I could see him, which also meant he could see me. Then, as often as I could, I'd shift back into third gear and pull away. When it worked, it was beautiful. It was my competitive edge message to him that said, "You're not going to beat me today." For any business to be successful, it must be competitively hungry. It's good to have a competitor that stokes your competitive fires. Everyone benefits.

Who can argue with the benefits of competition in business? You can get airfares today for roughly the same price as in 1980. Computers are

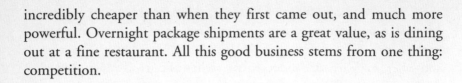

incredibly cheaper than when they first came out, and much more powerful. Overnight package shipments are a great value, as is dining out at a fine restaurant. All this good business stems from one thing: competition.

Desire by Respect

Desire also comes from having complete respect for your craft. For me as it related to racing, it wasn't just to win. It was to continuously figure out how to go faster. By respecting your craft, you have another source of desire. If you respect your craft, you are never satisfied with just winning. You have a hunger to continuously improve.

Dan Gurney was given a great brain for racing. He is one of the most innovative people I have ever met when it comes to creating more speed for a racecar. In 1970, I was driving for Dan Gurney's All American Racers Team. Our biggest competitor, McLaren Cars of England, had a lot more speed in their cars and we had to make up some serious ground if we were going to beat them. We were working feverishly on getting a couple of miles per hour more out of the Eagle racecars.

In the early 1970s, the racing industry figured out that the speeds we were running at were aircraft take-off speeds. The problem was we weren't flying airplanes. We were driving cars, and it was a good idea to keep the cars from lifting. First of all, if the car started to lift aerodynamically, we were in a lot of trouble. Second, the more we could actually force the car to stay down on the road, the better grip we had. The better the grip, the faster we could go. Our trick in auto-racing aerodynamics was not only to design the car to knife through the air to go faster, but to keep it from lifting off the ground. We had to aerodynamically reverse what the Wright Brothers created. Instead of lifting, we wanted to use aerodynamics to force the car down.

Auto racing was entering the field of aerodynamics, higher horsepower, and more sophisticated chassis designs. It was really becoming an expensive endeavor, especially when it came to the open-wheel Indy cars. Auto racing was also becoming much more popular for spectators, and television was generating huge audiences and revenues. The stakes were higher, and so was the investment to run a car competitively. It was getting to the point where another couple of miles per hour of speed would cost $50,000 to $100,000 to develop. If it meant winning the race though, it was worth it in prize money and sponsorship money.

By 1971, all the cars added wings for stability at the higher speeds. In our testing at Ontario early in 1970, we figured out that moving the wing back just another three and one-half inches was like adding 600 pounds of weight on the rear axle. This slight modification was one of our big secrets. That was good, but what Dan Gurney cooked up next was even better.

At a test in Phoenix, Dan hand-cut and shaped a couple of pieces of sheet metal that looked like angle-irons—just 90 degree bent pieces of aluminum. He had us mount them to the back edges of the rear wing on the car. I took the car out, went through the first turn and realized Dan had just made the biggest breakthrough in racing history! By the end of the day, after a few more modifications and test-runs, his simple "wicker-bill" invention—also known as the Gurney Flap—had given us another four miles per hour at the Phoenix International Raceway. We would not only beat our competition; we were going to beat them—and beat them bad.

The funny thing about this innovation was I immediately got paranoid and wanted to hide it. I scoured the stands and hills surrounding the Phoenix Raceway, looking for spies from McLaren, Penske, A.J. Foyt, or my brother, Al. I told our guys to hide these things immediately. Dan told me to relax. Leave them in the open. Don't bring attention to them. In fact, we went to Indianapolis that year and didn't hide them.

If you want to draw attention to something, try to hide it. By leaving the wicker-bill design out in the open at the 1972 Indy 500, we didn't draw any attention to it. It was there for everyone to see. It wasn't subtle, either. It was a piece on the wing and it wasn't even painted so it stood out like a sore thumb. But, nobody paid attention to the obvious. They were too busy looking for the hidden secrets.

In the 1972 Indy 500, that All American Racers Eagle really moved. It was the fastest car by a wide margin—in fact the widest margin in racing history. Up to that point, cars were topping out at about 178 miles per hour. My Eagle was running at 196 plus miles per hour, an 18 mile per hour advantage. Between the wicker-bill design and a secret turbocharger Dan Gurney acquired, we had the whole field beat by a huge margin. I led every lap of that race before the magneto shattered. The car was so fast that by the 25th lap I had already lapped my brother Al, who also had a fast car. The problem we ran into that day was we were pushing the envelope of speed and power out so far, that we created extra harmonic vibration in the engine. This harmonic vibration caused the magneto to shatter much like sound shatters glass. Once that happened, we were out of the race. The desire for more speed had driven us to a new level of performance in motor racing. Even though we didn't win, we sent a message to the racing world: We were the fastest by a wide margin, and the competitors didn't know where our speed was coming from.

People tend to get too caught up in winning as the only driving force to succeed. Winning is an objective, and naturally, it is a great thing to accomplish. However, if your only goal is to win, and you win, then what drives you? The craft is always bigger than any one win. No matter what you do in life, you can always get better, no matter how many times you win. You can't get to perfection, and that's the beauty of it. You can always improve. Improving your craft is a game that has unexpected turns and challenges. By challenging yourself to get better at your business, you are always looking for the new way to do things. It keeps the desire flowing after you've already taken home many trophies.

TURBOCHARGING YOUR OWN DESIRES

There are many sources of desire that can motivate you to achieve your goals. People use different types of desire to best create the fire in their bellies based on their circumstances. People who have reached material wealth status certainly do not have deprivation as a means for creating desire; instead, they'll use one of the other four sources to stoke their flames. Sometimes the source of desire changes as the mission unfolds. It could start out as being driven by deprivation, and then as the goal is approached it could be driven by a competitive desire. With five major resources fueling my desire—inspiration, deprivation, integrity, competition, and respect—I was never short of finding something to kick me into gear and take action to do something. I always had something to trigger my desire to achieve my goals.

Look for as many sources for desire that you can. Find inspirational people. Create more from less. Honor the principles of doing what's right by maintaining integrity. Pick a competitor who really fuels the fire in your belly. Have an unending respect for your craft so you will always be challenged to do better. The more ways you have to approach a problem, the more likely you are to solve it.

When you have the desire, you can accomplish anything. The fire in your belly creates a vision for your path. A picture emerges. The next step is to visualize your mission.

≣ PIT STOP POINTERS

- ■ Desire helps overcome obstacles.
- ■ Desire fuels your drive to the top.
- ■ Desire is triggered by:
  - • Inspiration—example of others.
  - • Deprivation—hunger fuels desire.
  - • Integrity—ensuring justice prevails.
  - • Competition—spirit of the human challenge.
  - • Respect—for the craft and its unending challenge to improve.

CHAPTER TWO

VISUALIZING THE CHECKERED FLAG

*I*ndianapolis 1963. This was my first Indy 500 opportunity, and in my
eyes it was going down the drain in a hurry. After Parnelli Jones cured
my homesickness with a good swift kick in my rear end, I ran into a new
obstacle. The best speed we could get out of owner John Chalik's car was
144 miles per hour, not good enough to qualify for the race. Parnelli broke
the 150 mph barrier. This was worldwide news—just like Chuck Yeager
breaking the sound barrier. Nobody had gone 150 mph in a racecar before!
That was unheard of! Several drivers subsequently ran over 150 miles per
hour for the first time in the history of the Indianapolis 500, and Parnelli
Jones had set the new track record at over 151 miles per hour.

Instead of doing more to get the car's speed up, Chalik decided to put a
grinding halt to the funds. We were out of tires, and he told me he wasn't
going to buy any more. It was Chalik's way of putting pressure on me to go
faster—to get performance out of me. I told him I needed more tires for the
practice runs. He told me to buy my own. I didn't have the money. Need-
less to say, we were at a standoff.

Parnelli Jones found me stewing on the pit wall with Chalik's mechanic,
Barney Christensen. He came over and asked me, "Why aren't you out on
the track practicing?!"

I told him, "Parnelli, I can't run. Chalik won't buy any more tires!"

Parnelli looked at Christensen and asked, "Is that true?!"

Christensen said, "Yep."

Parnelli wasn't about to let that issue sit still. He looked at me and Barney and said, "C'mon, Bobby! Let's go find another ride! You don't drive for this team anymore!"

My daddy kept pushing Parnelli into getting me a ride in the Novi; there was a yellow Novi just sitting there every day, begging for someone to drive it. It belonged to Andy Granatelli. Parnelli, in order to get Daddy off of his back, took me to Granatelli. "Andy, this is Bobby Unser," said Parnelli.

"Bobby who?!"

"Bobby Unser from Albuquerque. He's a good driver, and he needs a ride. You ought to let him take a run in your Novi. He'll do well."

Andy wasn't impressed. "Where's Albuquerque?!"

I responded, "It's in New Mexico."

Andy looked me over, "That Novi is a lot of car. What makes you think you are good enough to drive my car?"

Andy had a way of drilling you with his eyes when he talked to you—this was his litmus test to see if you were made of anything. He was pretty intimidating, and used this intimidation to overpower people in negotiating.

I told him, "I don't really know, but I think I'm good enough. I'd sure like to give it a try."

Andy scoffed, "If I let you take it out, you won't try to impress me? I don't want my car wrecked!"

The fact that Parnelli Jones was there made the difference. When Parnelli recommended somebody, it carried a lot of weight because he was the most successful driver in any circuit. I could tell just by the body language between Parnelli and Andy that Andy understood that Parnelli wasn't just backing me with his words—Parnelli knew I could drive the Novi.

"No sir, I won't." I replied.

"Okay. Get your helmet and your uniform, and we'll get your oil warmed up. You'll take it easy, right?" . . .

CONNECTING THE FIRE AND THE DREAM: CREATING THE VISION

While desire is certainly the fuel for success, it is not everything. Desire puts you in a position to be successful. It doesn't by itself guarantee success. Fuel in a racecar only guarantees that when the green flag is waved you have a good chance of going forward, not that you will go forward. There could be an accident, bad weather, or a mechanical failure with the car. A myriad of other issues come to play in order to become a winner.

Following desire, a critical attribute of winning is your ability to focus mentally on objectives and challenges. I'm not talking about setting goals, that will be discussed in the next chapter. I'm talking about the big picture, and realizing how critical a role your mind can play in anything. The mind can help conquer mountains like I eventually did at Pikes Peak. You accomplish this by learning how to visualize desired results. When you understand how powerful the mind can be, and how effective visualizing results can be, setting goals doesn't just become words on paper. Instead, visualization helps you create a mission with a vision, and through visualization, you'll fully realize that properly set goals *are* attainable. Once your mind has been actively trained through visualizing, it becomes stronger in another way as well. You'll find you will be able to react better to other catastrophic events that may arise. I like to refer to this as mental toughness.

WHAT IS YOUR VISION?

Imagine a job that you never grow tired of having. My ideal job would be driving the Pikes Peak Hill Climb race. I could do that all day, every day and never get weary. I've been dreaming it since I was eight years old. I'd go to bed at night dreaming about it, and wake up figuring out how I could make it happen. My daddy's brother, Louis Unser, lived in Colorado Springs and raced Pikes Peak every year. From the year I was born, 1934, until I was thirteen years old, Uncle Louis won the race nine times. He was the king of the mountain at Pikes Peak. Uncle Louis was my hero.

I dreamed about racing, but never had a chance to race until I was 15 years old. Daddy used to race with Bud and Jack Stagner out at the Cormit Speedway. He didn't drive the cars, but he furnished the super-modified pick-up truck body with a LaSalle flat-head engine. Albuquerque was the birthplace of super-modified racing. Daddy would let me drive the car to the race on race day. One day, his driver didn't show up. I bugged Daddy until he let me drive. I wound up taking fourth place in the main event. Well, that was that. The dream had become reality. I was hooked. From then on I couldn't race enough. My dreams of Pikes Peak had turned into clear visions.

In 1950, when I was 16, I went up to Pikes Peak to watch Uncle Louis practice for the race. That year, Uncle Louis had promised me that I would be able to drive his car back down the mountain after one of his practice days. I couldn't wait!

When I got to Pikes Peak the first day of practice, you can imagine the excitement in my 16 year-old mind. Pikes Peak! I will get to drive my hero Uncle Louis' car down the mountain! I visualized this so much that it's as though I was walking into my dream. I remember arriving at the mountaintop and looking for Uncle Louis. It was sunny and warm. The dust kicked up from the racecars was in the air.

I was up there with my good friend, Charlie Burger. We had no money, but I was willing to risk it just to be able to drive Uncle Louis' car down the mountain. Charlie and I found Uncle Louis, and he ignored me. Well, maybe he was just busy that day, and with a full week ahead of practice runs, there was plenty of opportunity.

Every day Charlie and I would go up the mountain, and every day Uncle Louis ignored me. He really upset me. He was definitely my hero, and here he had broken a promise. I would never do that to someone. I wouldn't even think of it. I've never knowingly turned down a fan's phone call or autograph request, let alone not saying hello to someone I knew or fulfilling a promise I made to them. Never.

On race day, I was up at the 16 mile mark waiting for Uncle Louis to race. Suddenly, I saw him come up out of Brown Bush Corner, and watched him take the turn at the 11 mile station toward Glen Cove. He wove his way past Elk Park and toward the turn where I was standing. He came around the turn. He wasn't pushing hard enough! He took the turn too careful. There was way more room for him to slide the car around the turn, which meant he could have been going a lot faster around that turn. I know this, because I pushed cars harder in the turns down at Cormit Speedway in Albuquerque. What was wrong with Uncle Louis? Doggone it, he ignored me all week, and I have to watch him come around this course as slow as that? C'mon! I can do better than that! Not only was the fire lit in me from all the nonsense he pulled during practice, but now I *knew* I could beat his ass in this race!

Then something suddenly struck me. I wasn't worshipping Uncle Louis anymore. I realized I was thinking about how *I* would win this race some day. All of the visualizing driving this race and experiencing the thrill of racing in Albuquerque came together as one thought: I would be *king* of this mountain some day! Uncle Louis' snubbing me had been the catalyst for this explosion in my mind. I told him after the race, "Uncle Louis, I'm going to be the new king of this mountain one day!"

I wasn't being arrogant. I knew from my experience racing at Cormit Speedway and my continuously visualizing the Pikes Peak race that I would do well. It was so deep in my mind and soul that I couldn't help but to see the end result: that I would be *king* of the mountain some day. It wasn't cockiness, either. It was a belief that I could visualize so clearly, even in my sleep. For many years since then, I have practiced putting my subconscious mind to work for me by visualizing results and goals as often as I can.

HOW TO VISUALIZE RESULTS

Early in my career, I learned to visualize situations and solutions. Visualizing situations helped me when issues would come up, such as accidents, and how to work around them. Visualizing solutions helped me develop new ways to do things better. Tonight, when you go to sleep, try thinking about improving your career. Make this a habit. Once this becomes a habit, you'll be surprised how often you'll wake up with creative ways to accomplish your goals. You think about solutions. It's not a worry; it's a dream that turns into reality by applying your continuous thinking to your daily activity.

When you're constantly thinking about solving new challenges and getting better at what you do, you never know when a creative thought will pop into your mind. You must be prepared for this. I always have some sort of recording device or pen and paper handy. Creative thoughts come in a flash, and disappear in a flash. Don't let them get away. I used to get some great ideas at 3:00 A.M., and occasionally would get on the phone with Roger Penske and go over them. Even though it was 3:00 A.M. in Albuquerque, it was 5:00 A.M. where Penske was in Reading, Pennsylvania. He was already up and working. Penske was another person totally devoted to working on improving his craft.

Like race drivers, successful CEOs have a never-ending passion to visualize results. Gordon Van Liew of Vita Fresh Orange Juice is an example of this. He was struggling with a trucking business in California in 1951 when he read somewhere that Houston was the nation's fastest growing city. His brother, Dell, had made it big in the orange juice business in California, so Gordon thought he would try orange juice in Houston. Gordon moved to Houston in 1952 and started the Vita Fresh Orange Juice Company with partner Art Becker.

Gordon was also a part-two local racecar driver. He used his racing ability to help fund the start-up of Vita Fresh Orange Juice. With only himself and Art to do all the work, they had many hats to wear. Six days a week, Gordon squeezed oranges, handled sales, and delivered the juice. On Sundays he would race to make money for the next week's bills. That type of driven vision went on for several years, until he and Art built Vita Fresh Orange Juice Company into the largest orange juice business in the South.

Gordon's real vision in racing, though, came to him in 1946, when he and his good friend, Dave Schneider, were listening to the Indy 500 on the radio. Gordon was so excited about the race, that at the end of the race, he turned to Dave and said, "Some day I'll have a car in the Indy 500!"

Gordon went to the 1962 Time Trials for the Indy 500. On Mother's Day, the Norman Hall car crashed and was for sale: car, starter cart, and trailer for $10,000. Gordon bought it on the spot and was now a car owner. The car, however, was too damaged to qualify for the 1962 race. The following year, 1963, Dempsey Wilson qualified the Vita Fresh Orange Juice Special for the Indianapolis 500. Seventeen years after vowing to bring a car to the 500, Gordon Van Liew broke down in tears as his vision was realized.

WHAT THE CONDITIONED MIND CAN DO

The mind can be very powerful. Using mine to its fullest has always been my number one priority as I worked to improve my racing career. Your mind, however is no different than your physical body—you need to condition it. I have found that the best way to condition the mind is by visualizing desired results. When you sleep, you can put your sub-conscious mind to work. This is free time for you to think.

There are many things we can see when we visualize ahead on our path to any goal. Obstacles, opportunities, work, confrontations, and so on—each one can be either a step forward or backward, a barrier or achievement. It's important not only to comprehend which, but also to understand that every goal has it's own set of circumstances, issues, and challenges to deal with. Being able to focus on objectives helps you keep your eye on the donut, not the hole. This stems from visualizing your desired results. Through such conditioning and effective use, your mind can help you:

- Identify what's important
- Conquer fears
- React properly to unanticipated obstacles

Identify What's Important

Being able to distinguish between the important and the unimportant is a vital skill, which stems from an ability to visualize and then focus on desired results. When I would lie in bed visualizing a race, I always saw myself focusing 100 yards down the track. That would give me about one second to adapt to a situation. I had to be aware of what was going on around me at all times. My peripheral vision would help me with what was happening on either side. My rearview mirror would show me who was making a move on me from behind. I had to see what was coming up immediately, otherwise I'd crash for sure. Through constantly visualizing these scenarios in my mind, I was able to react properly when the situation called for it. In fact, my reactions at times felt like they were natural because I had mentally rehearsed them so often.

In business it's the same way. You must focus on what's important. In most cases, that is the customer. When customers walk into your office or contact you, they are your spot 100 yards down the track. They become your number one priority. Any time you drop your focus from your customers, you may lose them and crash. When the phone rings, do you cringe or look forward to the call? Does it interfere with your work, or do you see it as an opportunity? If someone has taken the time to call, then it must be important. You never know when the next call will be the big break you need to really propel your business or career forward. Visualize your desired results at night, and you'll soon begin to notice you're moving toward your goals.

In my speaking and consulting work, one of the most focused people I have worked with is Knut "Ben" Bendixen of the Robert Bosch Corporation. He is the kind of person who walks into a room and is a presence without saying a word. It's not arrogance or flamboyance. Ben carries an aura of a dynamic, focused person. He's a confident force in his business dealings as well.

Ben came to the United States from Germany as a salesman in 1963 with Bosch. Over the years, through his focus and visualizing on the right things—paying attention to customers—he worked his way up the ranks. He became the National Sales Manager in 1982, the year Bosch got into auto racing. With success in sales promotion, he earned the Vice President of Sales position. Continuing his focus on customers and developing new markets, he became the President of Bosch USA, and finally the President of Bosch North America. Ben's efforts have given Bosch the reputation of quality and value in its many growing markets—automotive parts and audio equipment, appliances, power tools, and industrial equipment. By focusing on the right things, Ben

Bendixen has been the driving force behind Bosch North America's successful growth. I enjoyed watching a good man like Ben rise to the top.

It's critical to spend time focusing 100 yards down the track and learning how to focus on what's important. The more you visualize, the more likely you'll achieve your goals. Who would have thought a kid like me, growing up in Albuquerque, a city most people can't spell, would win three Indy 500s and thirteen Pikes Peak Hill Climbs?

Conquer Fears

I *had* to conquer my fear of flying and heights. Eighteen-hour drives every week to the California racetracks—Ascot and Imperial Valley— were killing me, physically and mentally. I had to drive back, too. I couldn't just leave my family alone in Albuquerque. I learned to fly, and, in the process overcame *some* of my fears of flying, not to mention I cut down my roundtrip travel time by a full 24 hours. I conquered my fears by visualizing myself flying an airplane, focusing out into the horizon, and landing safely at my intended destination. And by conquering those fears and anxieties, I had a much more positive focus to apply toward my racing.

When I raced Pikes Peak, I also had a fear of heights. I chose to focus on the race, not the fact that I was on the edge of a mountain. I used to practice driving the course in a passenger car extremely close to the edge at a real slow speed of about 20 to 30 mph. I did this just to become used to driving next to the sheer cliff drop-offs. I would visualize the entire course and how I would handle each turn, situation, and edge. I used my focus to simultaneously drive a great race and overcome my fear. If there's any one thing I learned from racing Pikes Peak, it's that if you concentrate during your visualizations on the objective, you can prevent your fears from paralyzing your progress. It's the same in business.

Some businesses let their fears overcome them. They're afraid to innovate because it may not work. They don't aggressively pursue more business because they fear they'll have too many customer service issues. When they get new orders, they see problems not growth. To be successful, you must overcome your fears. You must innovate, grow, and deal with issues in order to succeed. You need to spend time visualizing the success you can achieve by innovating and pursuing new business, not waste time and energy being afraid.

React Properly to Unanticipated Obstacles

Visualization can also help you prepare for unanticipated events. By visualizing possible scenarios and how you will react to them, you can prevent the unanticipated event from distracting you from your goal. You can't control sudden distractions, but you can visually prepare for handling them so they don't control you. Events you can't control are definitely not a priority because you can't do anything about them anyway. However, you can anticipate certain events. In racing, unanticipated events include car problems, accidents, or changes in weather. Pikes Peak was a great testing ground for unpredictable event preparation. The weather was constantly changing and would change dramatically during a 12-minute race to the top.

You're always going to have issues that foil the best-laid plans. That's just the reality of life. Something entirely unexpected will happen. You must prepare for this as best you can. It's good policy to do a situational risk analysis beforehand. Race teams do this before every race: they hold team meetings and discuss strategies and what-ifs to make sure everyone is focused not only on the same thing, but on the right thing. They also discuss what to block out, what things they can't control that they have to ignore or adapt to. We'll talk about strategy in more detail in the following chapter.

In 1964, my second Indianapolis 500, early in the race things were going great. I passed nine cars immediately in the first turn and six more down the back straight. I was looking for room to pass Johnny Rutherford, when all of a sudden 150 yards in front of us cars started spinning out. Dave MacDonald's car hit the inside wall, rupturing his fuel tanks and creating an incredible fireball. MacDonald's car then spun across the track to the outside wall, creating a wall of fire. It was the beginning of the worst accident in Indy 500 history. Eddie Sachs ran full on into MacDonald, killing Eddie and Dave instantly and creating more mayhem in the already horrific sequence of events unfolding in a split second in front of me. At 140 miles per hour, I had two seconds to stop or swerve.

I couldn't possibly stop the 2300-pound Novi loaded with 75 gallons of fuel in two seconds, and the inferno was wall to wall across the track. I couldn't go around it, either. I had one choice: to go *through* the wall of flame at full speed. It's like running your finger through a candle—if you do it quick, you won't burn. I was not about to let a full tank of racing fuel to get heated up for too long. The only problem was that there were definitely cars on the other side of that wall of flame, but I didn't know where.

I burst through the firewall at 140 miles per hour. Just as I came through the fire, I hit Ronnie Duman's car, clearing him of the fire, saving his life and managing somehow to keep myself straight. The crash had removed my front wheel and severed my steering and brake systems. I had no control whatsoever. Just then, Johnny Rutherford came out of the flames. His burning Watson/Offy flew over my hood. Somehow, I ground to a stop next to the wall on the front straight. It was my second Indy 500 and in just a couple of laps, I crashed and was out of the race. Stuff happens.

Businesses face similar issues. On May 25, 1979, an American Airlines DC-10 crashed shortly after take-off at Chicago O'Hare Airport. The left engine had fallen off its wing, rupturing the aircraft's hydraulic controls. The pilots couldn't regain control of the aircraft. Two hundred seventy-three people died in that crash. Because this was such a catastrophic event, the FAA went into high gear to determine the cause.

While they were investigating the crash, the FAA realized a number of DC-10s were still flying. At that moment, they had no certain cause of the engine mounting failure, so they had to assume that the potential problem existed with *all* DC-10s. The FAA grounded all DC-10s until the investigation could be completed.

At that time, Laker Airlines, the discount London to United States air carrier, had nothing but DC-10s in their air service. Consequently, the American Airlines Flight 191 crash and the subsequent grounding of the entire DC-10 aircraft fleet put Laker Airlines out of business for the time being.

The investigation by the FAA revealed that the maintenance procedure for removal and reinstallation of the engines recommended by the manufacturer, Douglas Aircraft, was not followed properly by any of the airlines that had DC-10s. The proper way to lift the engines to reinstall was with a sling. The airlines used forklifts, which could cause bolt thread-stress when not properly aligned. This missed detail in engine maintenance caused the crash. In fact, one airline had followed this procedure properly—Laker Airlines. They were shut down through no fault of their own. Just like the 1964 Indy 500 accident was not something I planned for, Laker Airlines was grounded due to something totally out of its control. Could Laker Airlines have possibly prepared for such an extreme circumstance? Hindsight is a wonderful thing, but foresight is a better way.

MENTAL TOUGHNESS

There is a difference between reacting to unanticipated obstacles that come up, and really bearing down with Herculean effort when faced with a huge challenge. This is where mental toughness comes into play. I found that my mental toughness was directly related to the amount of visualization I practiced. The more I practiced, the more mentally tough I became. Two challenges we face in life in which mental toughness comes into play are:

1. Major disasters
2. Financial challenges

Major Disasters

Mental toughness has helped me many, many times, particularly in racing in which each accident is a major disaster of some sort. Some of the ones I was involved in severely tested my mental mettle. In the late '50s, I started racing the bigger and more powerful midgets and sprint cars at Ascot in California and Manzanita in Phoenix. One race at Manzanita, I was at a midget car race, and made it to the trophy dash. During the dash, I was running second. Trying to pass the leader, my car's right rear slipped off the back straightaway. The car started flipping and cleared a huge irrigation ditch. I was so far off the track and out of the range of the lights that they had trouble finding me. When they finally found me, the car was upside down with the frame broken in half. I was unconscious and had a lot of broken bones. My thumb was resting on the red-hot exhaust pipe, burning the flesh severely.

The race was on a Saturday night. Bud Trainor, a good friend who helped me in the Phoenix races, was at the track and went with me to the hospital. The race organizers had arranged for any accident victims during the race to be transported to the cheapest hospital. I was lying in the emergency room, fading in and out of consciousness. It was like a medic's tent in a war: people were coming in with all sorts of problems—gunshot wounds, knife-wounds, beatings, and drug overdoses. I was just another number on the long list of dying patients.

I woke up once and I asked Bud, "Where's the doctor?" Bud replied, "Not here yet, Bobby." I passed out again. The next time I woke up, it was the same story. The third time I woke up, a nurse was standing there. Bud asked her to see if she could get someone to help me, and she replied matter-of-factly, "He's going to die anyway."

That's all I needed to focus on what was important. My mind instantly pushed through the pain. I grabbed Bud and said, "Get me out of here now!"

"Bobby, how do I do that?"

"Call an ambulance and have them come and pick me up and take me to another hospital."

"I don't have any money for an ambulance."

In reality, Bud was a very rich man, and probably had $500 in his pocket. He just didn't want to be embarrassed in front of the hospital people by calling another ambulance to take me to a different hospital. I was a little more interested in living than his being embarrassed.

"I'll pay for the ambulance. Get the phone book and make the call!"

"How are we going to get you out of here?"

"Just get the ambulance to come to the same place they brought me in, and push this whole damn bed down there and load me into it! Now go!"

The ambulance arrived. Bud pushed me, bed and all, down to the ambulance. They slid me from the bed onto the stretcher in the ambulance, and took me to the Methodist Hospital of Phoenix. The doctors there told me that if I had been another 20 or 30 minutes later in arriving, I would have died. There comes a point when you can really focus your mind through pain when the alternative is dying. I doubt I would have been able to do this if I hadn't spent so much time exercising my mind visualizing situations and objectives.

In the pre-dawn hours of January 17, 1994, Southern California was jolted awake with the 6.7 Richter-scale magnitude Northridge earthquake. Fifty-seven people were killed, and there were billions of dollars in damage done throughout the San Fernando Valley and the Los Angeles area. One area of devastation included West Los Angeles, where a section of the Santa Monica Freeway, Interstate 10, collapsed. Initial estimates were that it would take 18 to 24 months to fix the freeway. However, Governor Pete Wilson's office marshalled forces to expedite the repair work bidding process; it was done in two weeks, instead of months. The State government couldn't control the earthquake or what it did, but it controlled its own bureaucratic processes. It took serious leadership to do this.

Once the bids were complete, the winning contractor was given 140 days—less than five months—to complete the task. That was considerably less than the original 18 to 24 month estimate. There were incentives and penalties—$200,000 bonus per day to finish the work ahead of time, and $200,000 per day in penalties for missing the deadline. The contractor, CC Meyers, completed the work within 66 days—an unbelievable 74 days ahead of the deadline. CC Meyers earned an extra $14.8 million bonus.

The State government obviously couldn't predict the Northridge earthquake. But, after it happened, it had to gather, bear down, and fight through the challenge of a major commerce artery that was ruptured. It expedited the bid process, and was willing to pay out an extra $14.8 million in bonus money. The unacceptable alternative was to have a freeway out of commission, which the State estimated was costing the City of Los Angeles $1 to $3 million per day. The state officials focused through the pain of the earthquake and the unexpected expenses to overcome the obstacle.

It's not easy to think about the realities of life's unexpected challenges, but the sooner you learn to think about these tests and deal with them, the better it will be for you. I had to cope with some tough times early on. My brother Jerry died in 1959 at Indianapolis, and my brother Louis contracted Multiple Sclerosis in the early '60s. People say I'm cold, but I'm not, really. I just accept things as they are—good and bad. This allows me to keep things in perspective, and has kept the unexpected events from controlling me. I use my mental conditioning and toughness to continue the journey forward, despite the many, many obstacles and surprising challenges.

Financial Challenges

Money doesn't always motivate me, but I always fulfilled my financial obligations. I have never knowingly paid a bill late in my life, and I don't ever intend to. Whether you're motivated by money or not, you've got to pay your bills. In racing you don't get paid for your time you put in, although my experience has shown that the more time you put in, the more successful you will be. The real challenge of a racing career is to know that putting in time and a good effort isn't always good enough. You have to win to get paid. When bills were due, I *had* to perform. As any entrepreneur knows, it's a stressful feeling knowing you have to win to pay the bills, rather than winning for the passion of the race.

In 1959, I was married, had a house and two kids. I was responsible for my family. Preparing for the 1959 Pikes Peak Hill Climb, Daddy had a Jaguar engine in an open-wheel racecar built up that I was going to drive. Then an opportunity came up that I couldn't resist, but it put me in a financial bind. Denny Moore, Jack Zink's chief mechanic, called me. (Jack Zink was a big-time, wealthy racecar owner out of Tulsa, Oklahoma.)

Denny: "Bobby, Jack wants to get rid of this Pikes Peak car. It's the one your brother Louis drove last year. Why don't you buy it?"

I told him, "I don't have any money."

Denny: "How much have you got?"

I replied, "Just $1000. If I give you $1000, I won't have any money for gas to get to Tulsa to pick up the car."

Up to that point, I'd always been driving Daddy's car in the Pikes Peak Hill Climb. I still was going to drive his Jaguar-powered open-wheel car in the Open Division of the 1959 Hill Climb, but building my own car was really tempting. I couldn't drive two cars in the same division, but I figured I'd have my brother Al drive the Pontiac-powered car while I drove Daddy's Jag. Besides, Al was a good driver, and between the two of us, we were going to make some good money. I not only needed money for my family, I was looking at buying a cheap, old airplane so I could get to California racetracks in much less time than the 36 hours it was taking me to drive round-trip to California from Albuquerque.

Buying Jack Zink's Pontiac racecar was an opportunity for me to build and drive my own car, but I couldn't afford it. As often happens in life and business, when you have the slightest opportunity to take advantage of a situation, you go for it, because you don't know when or if that opportunity will ever come again. With Al driving my Pontiac engine car and me driving Daddy's Jaguar-powered car, the risk was worth taking. So I decided to go for it. For the $1000, Denny Moore gave me the frame, body, radiator, and a few other pieces. The problem was I didn't have any money to get back to Albuquerque from Tulsa, so Denny loaned me gas money as well. Now all I needed was an engine, rear end, and expenses to get to the race. Mere details.

At the time, it was standard for drivers and owners of cars to split race winnings 60 percent to the owner, 40 percent to the driver. Driving Daddy's Jaguar would get me 40 percent of the winnings, and Al driving my car would get me another 60 percent of his winnings. I had the opportunity to win a whopping $10,000 this time at the Peak. That potential paycheck was really looking good. The next trick was to get the other parts I needed to finish the car on payment terms.

Racecar drivers are notorious for not paying their bills. "You'll get paid if I win," just isn't something the parts suppliers want to hear. In fact, they hate it. However, one thing I had going for me was I was Jerry

Unser's son. Our family was known in the racing business as people who could be trusted to pay their debts on time. Daddy's relationship with the racecar parts suppliers in California was really helpful to me. Also, I was obviously following in his footsteps in the way I conducted my financial affairs as a businessperson, which allowed me to get 30 days terms with the parts suppliers. I never said, "If I win, you'll get paid." This never came up in conversation. So, although I had to be a cool cat on the surface, I was paddling like crazy underneath to make things happen so I could win that race.

Thirty days before the race, I started dealing with the California suppliers. I called Ted Hallibrand from Hallibrand Engineering to buy the rear end. At that time, Ted made all the rear ends in the racing business. Joe Hunt was the only person in the racing business who built quality magnetos, and Hillborn made all the racing fuel injectors. I called them and ordered my magnetos and fuel injectors. I told them up front that I didn't know how I was going to pay for this, but hopefully I would do well in the Hill Climb. They sent me the parts and gave me 30 days payment terms.

I still didn't have an engine, and for that I turned to the guy I was working for, Dick Hall. Dick Hall was an extremely wealthy person who inherited money in the oil industry, along with his brother Jim who was the developer of the famous Chaparral racecars. Racing was in their family. I built Pontiac stock car engines for Dick Hall in Albuquerque. I asked Dick if I could build an engine from various engine parts I had made up in his shop. He had no problem with me doing that, so I had the engine parts and spent my weekends building it.

I had a car to race, but I didn't have any money to get to Pikes Peak. Somehow, things always work out. This little, dinky motel on the West Side of Albuquerque on Highway 66, the Grandview Motel, heard about my financial dilemma. The owners gave me $1000 sponsorship money for the car. I had my own car, a good driver (Al), and a prime opportunity to win some desperately needed money.

We drove up to Pikes Peak a few weeks before the race with the two cars—Daddy's Jaguar-powered car and my Pontiac-powered car. Man, I'm telling you Al and I were really cooking—tearing up the practice runs. Things were looking good, but I was still worried, knowing I had to win to pay all these bills and feed my family. Then disaster struck the day before the race. Somebody ratted about Al's age. He was only 20, two months shy of his birthday and technically you had to be 21 to drive the Hill Climb. Now I'm in some serious trouble: Two cars, only one driver, and bills to pay. The only option left is to win.

I still had to figure out which car to race: Daddy's Jaguar-powered racecar, or my Pontiac-powered car. I felt strongly about the Pontiac—it had more horsepower and handled great. I thought it probably had the best chance of winning. Now Daddy had no driver for his Jaguar. So, I made a deal to give him 40 percent of the winnings—essentially giving him something for losing his driver, me—from what I won with my Pontiac-powered car.

On race day, my stomach was in knots. My head was exploding—I didn't know it then, but I had some serious sinus allergies so every time I went up to that pollen-laden, dust-filled road at Pikes Peak, my head ached. I was really determined to win—I had to. Losing was not an option. I focused through the pain and fears and roared through the Open Class race 13 minutes and 36 seconds, a new course record! I knocked a full 11 seconds off my own record set the year before, and beat the second-place finisher, Hill Climb veteran Slim Roberts by a full seven seconds. Now I could pay my bills, pay Daddy his winnings, feed the kids, and buy that old, used airplane to get me to more races! Incredible!

After the race, Barbara, my wife at the time, and I emptied our pockets and her purse onto the kitchen table in our cabin while we were laughing. It was all the cash we had to our name, and it was less than $1.00, but I had just won $8700! As tough as it was to win with the financial problems, with all the issues and the last-minute challenge that kept Al from racing, I used my ability to visually focus to drive my way through the challenge. Winning in this situation also reinforced my ability to perform under all kinds of pressure.

Manage All Other Challenges

You can't possibly prepare for every situation, but you can certainly rehearse how you will react. This keeps *you* in control, not the other way around. How many times do you find yourself in a reactive mode? Is it always? What is the cause of this? Is it because too many things are "going wrong," or is it because you're letting the things that go wrong take control?

In the business world, there's always going to be some key customer who quits buying from you for some reason. There's always going to be an unexpected merger, acquisition, or bankruptcy that changes the business landscape. A key employee will quit, or worse yet, die. If you are in business long enough, sooner or later these unexpected things will happen. How you react to these situations will depend on your mental toughness. Mental toughness is developed through a combination of mental preparedness through visualization, and actions that reinforce the vision in real experiences. We'll talk about taking action in Chapter 4.

Granatelli let me take his powerful Novi out for a run. They started the engine, and it thundered to life. Man, what a beautiful racecar! That was the most power I ever had in a car up to that point in my career. The crew chief gave me the thumbs up, I eased the clutch out and the Novi lunged forward. Just before I pulled out of the pits, Andy Granatelli leaned over and told me "Take it easy!"

I pulled onto the track, and the Novi handled like a charm. It was unbelievable! It had so much more power compared to Chalik's car! You've never been passed by a car until you've been passed by a Novi—it thunders past you and spits exhaust in your face as it roars by. That roadster could really haul ass! My third lap around the racetrack was 147 mph, and Granatelli was ready to wet his pants. He made a couple of adjustments to the windshield, and my next lap I ripped off at 149 miles per hour without any problem whatsoever. As I pulled back into the pits, Granatelli practically tackled me and kissed me, "You're hired!"

I qualified the car on the third day of qualifying, which was the second weekend, and qualified as the fifth fastest car out of the entire field of 33. That put me on the entire racing world's radar—I didn't have to explain to anyone who Bobby Unser was anymore. I was going to race in the Indianapolis 500! Now I was on the worldwide racing map. This was a huge jump in my career.

≡ *PIT STOP POINTERS*

- Visualization will sharpen your mental focus.
- With sharp mental focus, you can obtain objectives and overcome unanticipated challenges.
- Visualized solutions are spontaneous. Keep a pen or recorder handy for unexpected moments of inspiration.
- Mental toughness is developed by continually practicing mental focus on objectives and situational challenges.

CHAPTER THREE

QUALIFY FOR THE RACE
Goals and Strategies

W*e've worked so hard to get here; the mechanics, the crew, the engineers, and all the testing we've done. We started working toward the 1968 Indy 500 last September with a major meeting between me, our sponsor, the car owner, the head mechanic, and the chief engineer. We selected the engine and chassis then and started putting things together over the winter. Test after test after test. Chassis response, tire compositions, turbochargers, fuels—you name it, we tested it. Anything we could do to get more speed.*

Now we have to make all that hard work pay off. There's no more hiding. No more secret tests. We are out in the open and about to show the world everything we have been working on.

Gathering the whole race team for one last strategy is critical. We all need to be on the same page. What do we do, when do we do it, how do we respond to a competitor's strategy, and what do we do if something goes wrong? All this is discussed in detail—there is no more margin for error. This is the real deal.

We agree on our strategy, how we are to respond to certain situations, and who on the team is responsible for what. We're comfortable with the plan, and confident we are going to really do good today.

Winning the Indianapolis 500 was a lifetime achievement, not a short-term goal. I had been in over 600 races spanning twenty years before I won my first 500 in 1968. Heck, I had been racing for 15 years before I even *qualified* to race at Indianapolis! Winning the Indianapolis 500 was the result of achieving many other things first.

Everybody wants to win the Indy 500. They see the race on television, the glory of the Winner's Circle, the big endorsements, the smiles, and all the money. Isn't it great?!

Let me tell you, it isn't a ride in a chauffeured limousine you take to the top of the racing world. There are many losses, lessons, disappointments, crashes, and—yes, unfortunately—a few drivers die along the way. That's why racecar drivers are a different breed of athlete, and a different type of person. We know that as competitive as it gets, the fact that one of us may get severely injured or even die—in practice, testing, qualifying, or in the race—is all too real. We'll compete like hell with one another and fight among ourselves, but pity the poor bastard who tries to mess with a driver. Then he's got to take us all on. We'll talk about the racing family in another chapter, but for now, we'll focus on goals and strategies.

One of the reasons the racing world is so close-knit is we know how awfully hard it is to get to the top. Getting to the top—or getting to the finish of any race for that matter—requires another accomplishment first: you've got to qualify. You've got to *earn* the opportunity to compete. That means there are some prerequisites to take care of. If you want to qualify, you have to set some goals and develop a strategy to achieve those goals.

Once you have the fuel of desire and your mind is well-conditioned to accept challenges, the next step is to figure out where you want to go. For me, it was being the best racecar driver I could be, and supporting my family by doing so. The question I had to ask myself was, how do I really go about doing that?

Early on, I realized that the easiest things to accomplish are those that are totally within your control. Generally, the harder things are, the more likely they involve things out of your immediate control. Look at how many things are out of a racecar driver's control in order to win a race: the car, the pit crew, the competitors, the competitor's pit crew,

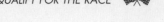

the track, the weather, and so on. It's almost enough to make you want to retire before you even start.

Naturally, the ultimate objective for any racecar driver is to win races. But with so many things out of your control, the odds of winning any given race are incredibly small. I devised a simple building block system approach to reaching the ultimate goal of winning races. The system is based on conquering first that which is most in my control. I thus divided racing into three components: go fast, lead, and win. In that order.

The thing I had the most control over was how fast I drove the car. That was totally up to me, especially in practice and qualifying when there's only one car on the track. Qualifying is when there are the fewest outside influences. Thus, going fast became my first priority. Once I was able to go fast, my confidence increased enormously and I caught the attention of sponsors. I hadn't won any races yet, but I had set an attainable goal for myself that was totally within my control.

Once I was able to go fast, I then set my sights on the next objective—lead the race. Leading in a race certainly requires the ability to go fast, but other factors now come into play that are outside your control, namely your competitors. After capturing the lead in a race, I'd then shift my goal to leading for a lap, then two, and so on. I lost many a race in which I led for an instant, a lap, two, three, and more. When my sights were set on going fast and leading, I certainly felt like a winner, especially given the increased attention I was receiving from sponsors, team owners, and fans.

After accomplishing my interim goals of going fast and leading, I then knew I could win races.

SETTING YOUR GOALS

Unfortunately, many people think all they have to do is set the goal, and somehow they'll achieve it, as if by magic. They forget about all the hard work that's required. If you want to become CEO of General Electric, you don't jump over the fence and move into Jeff Immelt's office. There's a long, hard road you have to take to get there. You have to achieve quite bit before you *earn* the right to move into the corner office, just as a driver has to earn the right to race at Indy.

The reality of qualifying for the Indy 500—not only as the ultimate goal following many, many other achievements—is also an intensely competitive process. Before you are even given a driver's test at the Indianapolis Motor Speedway, you must have a number of major driving accomplishments under your belt.

First, you must have won many races in whatever race circuit series you compete in, something more competitive than the Saturday night stock-car races. The races must be recognized and sanctioned by a responsible racing organization. You can't just win one race; you've got to show consistent competitive performance in your circuit—you must excel in your race circuit. Excelling means you started many races, finished many in the top five spots, and you had to be a season point winner in your racing circuit. That means you finished in the top of several races throughout your race season to win more points than any other driver.

Next, other proven Indianapolis 500 drivers must recommend you. Parnelli Jones recommended me because he watched me race many times in California. Indy racing is so incredibly dangerous that this can't be a popularity contest. They only recommend people they can trust to handle the super-high horsepower cars—anywhere from 600 to some over 1000 horsepower, at very high speeds in heavy traffic for three and a half hours. Finally, you can't take the test unless you have a car. So, you need someone who is willing to put up a million or so dollars to give you a ride. It's unfortunate at this point, because there are good drivers who just don't have the financial backing to afford this part of the qualification. Money doesn't buy you into the 500, but it could buy you an opportunity that others didn't have. Money can buy you opportunity, but it can't buy you desire. In the end, it's the drivers who really have the desire to drive that ultimately win, not the ones who try to buy their way in.

Once you have the proven racing record, the recommendation of some respected Indy 500 drivers, and a million dollar ride, you now get to take the test. It's no Department of Motor Vehicles test, either. You have to schedule the test with the Indianapolis Motor Speedway and

Race Officials. Many Indianapolis 500 drivers watch you take this test—they're the judges. They are stationed around various parts of the two and a half mile oval racetrack. You start out by running laps at a set speed, maybe 150 miles per hour to start. The drivers watch to see if you know the lines you need to run through the turns. Do you start into your turn properly and pull out into the straight on the right lines? Are you consistent? Then you're asked to increase the speed and go through the same evaluation process. Can you control the car at different speeds consistently through the racetrack? They are all judging you, and if you don't cut it in their minds, you're not going to pass. It's like selecting astronauts for NASA—the judges don't have to tell you why you failed.

By now, you can see that you have to be quite an accomplished and confident driver before you get to Indianapolis. I didn't try to qualify until I was 29 years old. I had already been racing 15 years and had been in over three hundred races before I got my first test-drive at Indianapolis. Once you qualify to *drive* the Indianapolis 500, you're still not qualified for the race. There are only 33 cars in each Indianapolis 500, but there are approximately 60 drivers and over 80 cars available to qualify for the race every year.

The Indianapolis time trials are the last leg of your journey to make it to the 500 on Memorial Day weekend. The trials are run the first two weekends in May. You get to run three warm-up laps and then you run four qualifying laps by yourself. The average speed of the four qualifying laps is calculated. After that, you have to sit back and wait, and hope that your time is one of the top 33 out of everyone qualifying.

KNOWING YOUR LIMITATIONS

There were plenty of races at Indianapolis I knew I didn't have a chance in hell of winning. This could have been because the car I was driving was just not running fast enough to win, or because someone else came in with a car that was running so much faster than anyone else. This has to be put in perspective. A car that will go 194 miles per hour versus a car that will go 192 miles per hour has a significant advantage. It may appear to be only two miles per hour, but over a 200-lap, 500-mile race, that's two laps, or five miles. A two-lap advantage in speed alone before the race starts is a significant advantage.

With a slower car, any objective going into the race was to do better than we should do. From the 1963 through the 1966 racing seasons, the cars I was driving just weren't going to compete with the other cars. The best we could hope for on a great day was a fourth place finish. That didn't deter us from racing or improving everything we could to milk another mile or two per hour out of that machine. Jud Phillips was the crew chief, and one of the best ever. I was really fortunate to get hooked up with Jud and Little Red (Tom) Herrmann. They did a great job setting the car up, and I did my best driving it. That's all we could ask of ourselves, but doing this did set the table for future success.

PRIORITIES

It's worth delving into more detail about the importance of prioritizing. As I've explained, my first priority was always that which was in my immediate control. Another word for *going fast* would be *improve*. Set as one of your primary goals to improve whatever it is you are doing. People notice when you continuously do things better. And what's easier to improve than that which is in your immediate control? Despite my early crash in the 1963 Indy 500, I went fast enough to grab the attention of Gordon Van Liew, president and founder of the Vita Fresh Orange Juice Company, a big-time racing owner. Once Gordon saw I could go fast, he realized I had a chance to win. He provided the racecars and funds for me for the following season.

As we learned, the faster we went, the more positive attention we received. The closer to the pole we got, the more prerace press we would attract. And more press and attention invariably led to more sponsors, which meant more money and better equipment.

Many businesses have grand-opening promotions to grab customer's attention and, it's often the one type of marketing promotion that's most in their immediate control. Krispy Kreme Donuts has become a master of grand-opening promotions, with some stores generating as much as $400,000 in business in the *first* week. (The average Dunkin' Donuts generates about $750,000 in an entire year.) Talk about getting attention! A Krispy Kreme grand opening isn't an advertised event—it's local news. They start incredibly fast, and get a lot of attention. Then they keep customers coming back for more with their famous "HOT" light, telling customers to come on in for fresh, hot donuts. As a result, Krispy Kreme's corporate performance improves, and that attracts more investors. Go fast, lead, and win.

Once you have captured the attention of the fans by performing well in the short-term, you can leverage that into long-term successes. In my first three Indy 500 races, I went fast, but didn't get too far. In 1963, the crash into the wall put me out of the race early, and I wound up finishing dead last—in thirty-third place. I had to plow through the biggest fire ever at the 1964 Indy 500 after only a few laps, but considering two drivers—Eddie Sachs and Dave MacDonald—were killed in that accident, being alive and not winning wasn't so bad. In 1965, qualifying with the eighth fastest time to put us in the third row for the start grabbed more attention. Things were going great in the race until an oil fitting broke on the sixty-ninth lap, finishing me nineteenth. With the fast speeds getting everyone's attention—not just the fans, but the mechanics, sponsors, and owners—it was time I figured out the next step—how to finish.

After a business has grabbed someone's attention with its grand-opening promotion, then the business needs to leverage that success. As hard as it is to get to this point—all the planning, trials, tribulations, and anxieties—now comes the really tough part: delivering on your promises. Talk is cheap. Now you've got to deliver. So far, Krispy Kreme has been delivering.

In 1966, I raced for Bob Wilkie's Leader Card Race Team and the ace-veteran mechanic Jud Phillips and his great number two mechanic, Tom Herrmann (Little Red). I was on a vastly improved team then and changed cars from the Novi roadster to a rear-engine Gerhardt. We still weren't going to blow the field away, but we went faster and deeper into the race. That year an eighth place finish at Indy and still running at the end of the race proved our ability not only to go fast, but to go the distance. The equipment and the team were coming together. We shifted from just qualifying fast and leading to getting better equipment to go faster and longer. The next step was to get a car that we could win with.

That happened in 1967, when Jud Phillips and I convinced Bob Wilkie we could win with one of Dan Gurney's Eagles. On July 1, 1967, we won our first two road races at Mosport. We finished second or third in six more races that year. Leader Card Team had a breakout year in 1968. Starting with a win on March 31 at the Las Vegas 150, we ran off a string of four consecutive wins, culminating with my first win at the Indy 500. It took five years to go from a dead-last finish to a win at Indy, but I made it by seeing the big picture the whole way, and taking it one step at a time.

PREPLANNING

Looking back, the key to my reaching any goal or objective has been advance preplanning. Preplanning comprises two elements: homework and strategizing. Regardless of how much I may have wanted to go fast, if I didn't spend the time planning how I was going to do it, the goal setting in and of itself would have been a total waste of time. It was so important for me to conduct prerace planning. It wasn't just a matter of thinking about the plan and what to do. What I did was actively plan. To increase your chances for success, you have to investigate, research, and increase your knowledge base—in other words—do your homework.

One time after I had retired from racing, I got a call from a fellow in Edmonton, Canada. He wanted me to do an ice race. I didn't want to do it. I had never done an ice race before, and I didn't have any interest in doing one then. I politely refused, and ended the conversation. However, for some reason I took down his phone number. I had second thoughts, and decided to call him back.

"Tell me about your ice race. I've never done one."

He replied, "Well, we've got a lake, we take bulldozers and graders and make a road course out of it."

"What would I do for a car?"

He said, "We'll get you a car."

"What divisions have you got?"

He answered, "We've got every division from no-studs to cars with big studs on their tires."

"I'd like to run a fast class race—I assume it's going to be the big-studded tire race."

He said, "That's right."

We discussed the fee and arrangements. I told him I needed a round-trip airline ticket. I didn't want to be embarrassed, and if I got up there and they were going to give me a bad car and humiliate me, I was going to jump on the next plane back from Edmonton to Albuquerque. I was committed—I won't do anything if I think I'm going to be set up to lose. He assured me that I'd have a competitive car.

I thought more about the ice race and figured it would be just like racing at Pikes Peak, except on ice. I flew up to Edmonton. There were really nice people running the ice race, and they were happy to have Bobby Unser come up and drive in these frigid conditions. I got out to the lake, got in my car, and took it out on the course. Within five minutes I knew I was going to really do well. But even that wasn't good enough, because I knew the car could do more. So I became really friendly with the mechanic, and had him make a few setup adjustments for me.

I went out on race day and just kicked everybody's ass in every race I ran—I won everything and set new records. They started the race inverted—the top qualifier goes last—and since I was the top qualifier, I went last. I won every race I was in, including one that I flipped the car and broke out my windshield. The main reason I won these ice races, which I had never done before, was because I actively planned. I did my homework. Of course, just doing homework in and of itself is not enough. You have to take what you learned from investigating, and create a well thought-out strategy.

STRATEGY

Nowhere in racing is strategizing more important than at the Pikes Peak Hill Climb. It is the second oldest race in the United States, second only to the Indianapolis 500. In the racing profession, it's as prestigious as the Indy 500. As much as I was not so confident to race Indy back in

1963, I always *knew* I could compete in the Hill Climb. I had a burning desire to race the Pikes Peak Hill Climb, and the confidence to win. But that wasn't enough. I also had to have a prerace strategy.

Pikes Peak presents some very unique challenges to a racecar driver. Each year the number of races and categories could change. This would change the number of cars competing. Since the cars ran the course one at a time, you could start early in the day, or late in the afternoon.

If you raced early in the day, you probably were going to have good weather. However, with an early start, the road conditions weren't as good. There was a lot of loose gravel and rocks, which would cause you to slip. As the day progressed, the loose rocks were thrown off and you'd get better traction. However, later in the day you had to contend with afternoon thunderstorms, which often brought hail and a thick cloudbank to drive through on the way up.

The weather and road conditions were two critical factors to consider when trying to figure out your qualifying plans. Since a driver doesn't pick his start time for the race—start times are based on where they qualify—this necessitates a little more planning. Unlike the Indy 500, where you want to qualify first to gain everyone's attention and start the race in front, you may not want to qualify fastest in the Hill Climb. If the top qualifiers go early on race day and the weather forecast shows it's going to be good in the afternoon, then you don't want to go early. Depending on how the Hill Climb set up the rules on whether the fastest qualifier goes first or last, I'd change my qualifying strategy based on when I wanted to run—early or late.

Some years I didn't want to qualify the fastest so I could take advantage of my race starting time. I know this is a departure from my normal strategy to qualify fast, but at Pikes Peak qualifying fast wasn't as important as winning. All kinds of variables and schemes come into play when you're trying to gain the best advantage to reach your goals. With a sound, carefully reasoned strategy, you'll increase your chances to succeed.

Wouldn't life be grand if everything always went as planned? However, in my entire racing career, I never ran a race that went as planned. For that reason, there are a number of contingency aspects to goal setting and strategizing that need to be discussed.

ADAPTIVE STRATEGY

As soon as any race started, everything we assumed would happen changed. The importance of a prerace strategy became ever more clear. However, winning one race like the 500 isn't the only thing that's going on in the racing business. There's also a *race season* that ends in the fall. The challenge in planning for the race season is that the main event—the Indy 500—is held in the beginning of the season. It's like playing the World Series in May, then playing the rest of the baseball season. With the biggest single sports event early in the race season, race teams have some interesting challenges developing strategies. Some teams have to adapt their season strategy while looking at next year's 500 as the season unfolds. For example, if one team had an opportunity to win the race season, it would do whatever was necessary to win each race. However, if the team had one or two bad races, and were suddenly out of reasonable contention for the championship, the team would modify its goals and set its sights on developing a faster vehicle for the next year's 500. Plans are always changing.

Whatever strategies are adapted during a race or throughout a race season, there is one simple fact: *the teams that can adapt the quickest are the ones that win.* The teams that adapt the quickest are the ones that have a carefully planned prerace strategy.

On April 13, 1970, at 9:08 P.M., 200,000 miles from earth, Jack Swigert on board Apollo 13 uttered the six most understated words in aerospace history: "Houston, we have a problem here." An explosion had occurred, severely reducing the available oxygen and power to the craft and crew. The crew had to move into the Lunar Module until just before earth re-entry, some 90 hours later. To conserve power, they shut down the Command Module, waiting to power it back up just prior to re-entry. The crew of Jack Swigert, James Lovell, and Fred Haise had to reduce their electric power consumption and personal water consumption to one-fifth of normal. Just prior to re-entry into the Earth's atmosphere, the temperature in the Command Module dropped to 38°F. Prior to powering it up, NASA engineers had to work intensely for three days to write a workable procedure. Normally this procedure would take three months.

Working to solve the problem, NASA engineers and the crew on Apollo 13 took what they knew they had left of the Apollo 13 equipment and supplies, and adapted their strategy to bring the astronauts home safely. NASA classified the mission as a successful failure because of the safe return of the crew. As I said, the teams that can adapt are the ones that win. NASA is no exception.

CONTROLLING DIVERSIONS

Setting priorities and developing a strategy is great, but you'll always have diversions. Sometimes, you'll wander too far in your vision or off-track. If you know that distractions can occur and learn to prepare for them, you won't lose your way as often. Key elements to apply are:

- Avoid sidetracks
- Don't look too far ahead
- Modify goals after failure

Avoid Sidetracks

In the late 1970s, some open wheel (Indy) race teams thought Formula 5000 was going to be the way to go. So they abandoned their Indy car development and jumped on the "5000" bandwagon. It failed and put a few people out of business. They lost focus and got diverted.

Many people, especially recent college graduates, get misled early on in their careers when they take any opportunity that comes along. They wind up getting diverted off of their long-term path. They take a job for the paycheck without thinking about their career path. Then they move from job to job with no continuity in their direction. After a few years, they've had many positions, but they haven't gone anywhere.

Even big businesses sometimes sway off course. In the 1980s, Exxon Oil bought Reliance Electric. Oil not only doesn't mix with water, in this case it didn't mix too well with electric motors. Eventually, Exxon sold Reliance and refocused on oil. Many more companies have thought that they can just buy anything and turn on their corporate magic and everything will work. Well, nothing works by itself, and every

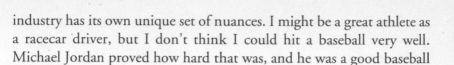

industry has its own unique set of nuances. I might be a great athlete as a racecar driver, but I don't think I could hit a baseball very well. Michael Jordan proved how hard that was, and he was a good baseball player. He happened to be a more focused basketball player.

Don't Look Too Far Ahead

A major problem can occur if you look too far ahead. You can't think about Pikes Peak in July when you're preparing for Indianapolis in May. You have to focus on the immediate task. The great thing about auto racing is when you are in a race, you cannot afford to think of anything else except driving hard at that moment.

Like sports teams that get beat by *this* week's patsy by thinking too much about a bigger game *next* week, businesses get caught all too often by looking too far down the road. For example, it's good customer service to deliver a product on time. It also happens to be good for the business, because the company gets paid for what it delivers. What suffers when a business is *only* focused on shipping product on time? Quality. While the on-time shipments help with establishing a good reputation for on-time delivery and good cash flow, it could sacrifice the quality reputation and cost money in returns.

This was a big problem for many years in the 1980s at Harley-Davidson. It was more important for the production workers to get product out the door than it was to get it right. What happened? All you saw around the country were people nearly breaking their legs trying to get their defective Harleys kick-started. What kind of product quality testimony is that for people? They were going the way of the Yugo.

Finally, Harley-Davidson figured it out: Get it right first. Get it out the door second. Then, do it better and do it again. By focusing on the right goals in the right order, Harley-Davidson has become a major turn-around business success story.

Modifying Goals after Failure

As a race progressed, if things went wrong—a problem in a pit stop, engine problems, an accident that put us way behind—we had to modify our goals. Sometimes, I would tinker with a car before a race, and actually make it run worse. That happens. What do you do when things don't go right? How do you adapt your goals?

One thing is for sure—we don't have the benefit of instant replay in life. When an event happens, it happens, and no matter how many times you run the replay, it doesn't change the outcome. Time marches forward. If we don't make the first goal when we wanted to make it, then we have to adapt to the fact that achieving the goal will have to wait. The most critical thing about modifying goals after a failure or a missed deadline is to not give up. The worst thing that can happen with a failure is that you'll learn something. We'll talk in much greater detail about failure in a later chapter, Cherish Failure.

Your road to success starts with a burning desire to succeed at whatever you do. Then you have to visualize a clear objective, plot a course consisting of small objectives that lead to the ultimate prize, and create a workable and flexible strategy. The next step is to take action.

≡ PIT STOP POINTERS

- Goals give your desire direction.
- Identify your ultimate objective.
- Plot a series of interim objectives.
- Prioritize your interim objectives in order of most within your control to most not within your control.
- Preplanning is essential.
- Develop strategies with contingencies in mind.
- Adapt and modify plans if goals have changed.

CHAPTER FOUR

START YOUR ENGINES!

I was always nervous before the start of an Indianapolis 500. I was so nervous in the first one in 1963 that I forgot to pee before the race. In my nineteenth and last 500 in 1981 I was so nervous I still forgot to pee before the race. There are approximately 400,000 people at the Speedway and at least 100 million more watching on television. We're in million-dollar plus cars, driving them over 200 miles per hour, with thirty-two other drivers trying to accomplish the ultimate goal in racing—winning. I don't care how many races any driver has raced in or won, at the start of the 500 everybody's nerves are rattling.

Then something happens that changes everything. We've been planning, strategizing, practicing, and scheming to do whatever we can to prepare for this event—to reach this ultimate goal. Then four words pierce the air at Indianapolis that switch the nervous energy to focus: "Gentlemen, start your engines!" In that instant, with the roar of 33,000 horsepower coming to life, I know that the real journey is about to begin. This is the moment years and years of work comes to—hundreds of races, many crashes and disappointments, highs and lows—all of the emotional energy of that long, hard road is switched to total focus and action. . . .

Once you have desire, can visualize success, and have a strategy to achieve your goals, it's time to get things in gear. A lot of money, and thousands of hours of fabricating and testing are put into building a racecar, but nobody learns anything until they're in a race. This chapter will focus on taking action—cranking the engine up, letting out the clutch, and pushing the car to its outer limits.

Taking action accomplishes several purposes: It shows you to be a person of initiative. It helps build self-confidence. It gives more meaning to your words. In the end, people respect those who take action.

Of course, taking action doesn't mean doing so half-cocked without adequate forethought. It means doing so strategically and clarifying key issues. I love to ask questions, and I'll keep asking until I fully understand whatever is unclear. Looking back, much of my success on and off the track was due to my persistent ability to ask questions.

Since I retired from racing, I have been involved with many business activities. One of these activities is as an expert witness for automobile and racing-related lawsuits. The first case I was involved with was a wrongful-death lawsuit brought against Chrysler in a racing accident. The autopsy revealed that the driver died from a broken neck. The family of the driver was the plaintiff suing Chrysler. Through their "expert" witness—a degreed and professionally licensed engineer—they claimed that the Gelcoate on the driver's helmet was ultimately responsible for causing his death. Gelcoate is a coating that goes on the helmet, much like paint. Without getting into the details, the plaintiff's engineer said in depositions that the Gelcoate was so strong that it could withstand several thousand pounds of force before breaking.

Pete Durney, the defending attorney for Chrysler, hired me to help with their case. Naturally, I asked Pete a lot of questions. How did the accident happen? What did the autopsy reveal? What safety gear was the driver wearing? What was the plaintiff's claim against Chrysler? How did the plaintiffs back up their claim? May I see copies of the depositions? After asking many, many questions and reviewing the facts thoroughly, I realized there was no legitimate claim that the strength of the Gelcoate could have possibly caused the injury per the plaintiff's expert witness.

When the case went to trial, and the "expert" engineer witness was under cross-examination, he was asked, "How much force can the Gelcoate withstand?" Since he had already answered this question in a deposition, he couldn't change it in court. He replied, "Several thousand pounds." At this point, I took the helmet in question, held it so the jury could see, and flicked off a piece of the Gelcoate with my fingernail. Questions asked, answers given, facts assembled, case dismissed.

I used to ask tons of questions at the prerace drivers meetings. It would make the other racers absolutely crazy. But I was adamant about seeking clarification on the ground rules before a race, especially because rules change right up until race time. Other drivers could ask these questions, but they didn't and usually just sat there and listened. By asking questions, I completely understood what the rules meant. Sometimes, my questions would lead to arguments. More often than not, I became the main benefactor of the knowledge gleaned from these sessions.

When you start taking action and get accustomed to doing so, you'll begin to notice a number of things. First, you'll become aware that you have greater control of your destiny. Then you'll notice that you have more power to dictate the terms of your dealings. Your confidence will grow as your experience increases. Finally, you'll learn to attack and solve problems more efficiently.

TAKE YOUR FOOT OFF THE BRAKE

Nobody ever achieved a goal until he started his journey. I never won a race with my foot on the brake. We had brakes on our cars, no doubt, but they were only used so we could gain an advantage in the race. In Indy cars, we used brakes to slow us down coming into the pits, waiting until the last seconds to brake hard before pulling into our pit area. With midget and sprint cars, we would use brakes to get the car to handle better through turns, applying the brakes as we went into the turn to get the car to bite in on the track so we could accelerate more quickly coming out. Other than helping gain more racing track time with the Indy cars, or better performance through turns in midget and sprint races, we seldom used brakes except in road racing, where brakes are used extensively. If you want to win a race, your foot must be on the accelerator.

Taking your foot off the brake means you've got to take initiative. In 1959, after I won the Hill Climb with my first car (the one I bought parts from Jack Zink and built with the Pontiac engine), I realized I needed more parts for my Pontiac race engine. I figured the best place to get these parts was from Pontiac itself. Of course, I didn't know anyone there personally, and figured they never heard of me either. But I really needed those parts. So, I picked up the phone and called Detroit, Michigan and asked for the Pontiac Division of General Motors.

I knew there was a man named Bunky Knutsen who ran the General Motors Pontiac Division. By sheer luck and somewhat of a miracle, I got through to his secretary who put me through to him. I said, "Mr. Knutsen, my name is Bobby Unser from Albuquerque, New Mexico, and I run Pikes Peak Hill Climb. I just won the race here (1959)."

He answered, "I know that."

"My problem is that I need some parts for my Pontiac race engine: a cylinder block, a crankshaft, some cylinder heads. Maybe, Mr. Knutsen, you could assist me in getting a few engine pieces. They don't have to be new, just pieces I can use to build an engine with," I continued.

He said, "Well, Bobby, I don't know what we can do, but let me call over to engineering and let me see what we've got."

I didn't want to push a man of his rank on the telephone. I just told him what I wanted and hoped things would happen. Personally, I thought nothing was going to happen, and that I'd never hear from him again. A few weeks later, I was working in my shop in Albuquerque, and a huge semi-trailer truck pulled up out front. The driver walked in and said, "Where do you want these?!"

I said, "What have you got?"

"I've got some engines for you," he replied.

We went out to his truck and he opened the trailer and it was full of Pontiac racing engines, three high from the front to the back! All new! There must have been 45 engines in there! Heck, all I needed was parts from about three engines, and I would have been really happy. Forty-five!! I had more engines than I knew what to do with. I kept ten, and gave the rest away to locals for racing. I didn't even have a place to store them so I had to get rid of most of them anyway.

Any time you become a person of action, people notice. They notice what you do, and more importantly, they will listen to your words. By providing the engines Bunky Knutsen proved this point. He became a great friend to me. Woody Allen was close when he said "70 percent of success in life is showing up." It's all about showing up and taking initiative.

USE YOUR ACTIONS TO BACK UP YOUR WORDS

I like to do business in a simple fashion: a handshake. You say what you will do, commit to doing it, shake hands, then go do it! It's that simple. I know things are much more complicated today, and business deals require contracts and sometimes lawyers, but when you take actions that back up your words, you really make things easier in the long run. Bob Wilke did business on a hand shake. His word was his bond, and everybody knew this. Over the course of many years, people who did business with an honest hand-shake went with Bob. That's how he got good people like Jud Phillips and Little Red Herrmann, and why I resisted the Granatelli's intense pressure to drive for them in 1968. You'll hear more about that story later in the book.

The first year I went to work for Roger Penske, I quit the team on the second day of testing over a clear misunderstanding of what we had agreed on verbally. The race season had just ended in 1978, with the last race in Phoenix. We raced hard Friday, Saturday, and Sunday. When the race ended on Sunday, I was officially done racing for Dan Gurney, and Roger Penske released Tom Sneva. So now I was with Team Penske, and dog-ass tired after racing three days. Penske wanted some testing done, and wanted to start right away on Monday. He was my new boss, and I wasn't going to let him down. As tired as I was, I put in a full day of work on Monday in Phoenix testing new wings.

What I really wanted to get going on was the new car Penske had promised me I was going to test. He said I'd be able to do some testing in Ontario, on the next day, Tuesday. Ontario was the best place for testing. It was a smooth track with little wind. Best of all, Ontario was a 2½ mile oval track, a duplicate of the Indianapolis Motor Speedway. The whole race team and I packed up and dragged our sore, tired bodies over to Ontario, California.

I was expecting to drive the new Penske car, which was really the only reason I went to Ontario right after a hard race. Then Jim McGee set me up in Sneva's car, whom I had been racing against—and beating, no less—just two days before. "What's this all about?" I wondered. I was supposed to see the new car and start testing it. Why did Jim roll out Sneva's old car? Then I figured it out: he wanted to see if I was faster than Sneva. Well, why in the hell did they hire me to begin with?! Wasn't the fact that I'm faster the reason I was hired *before* going to Ontario? The agreement I had with Penske was for me to start testing the *new* car. Well, that was that. I told Jim I quit, and got in my car and headed to the hotel.

Just as I was exiting the Ontario Speedway, guess who's pulling in? Roger Penske. He asked me, "Where are you going?!"

I said, "To my hotel, then to Albuquerque. I quit."

"Why?!"

"Roger, we had a deal: I was to come out here to do testing on your new car. McGee's just trying to see if I'm faster than Sneva. I proved that before you hired me. You need to hire another driver."

"Where's your hotel? Just give me two hours and I'll meet you in the bar. We'll work this out."

Sure enough, Roger Penske worked things out with Jim and the rest of the Penske team as to what my role was, especially in testing and development. By sticking to my words, and just as importantly, backing them up with credible actions, I was able to make sure things happened the way I had intended. When your actions back up your words, then your words have real meaning. As a result, you begin to have greater control over your destiny. By the way, Jim McGee and I became the best of friends. I really liked working with him after that incident.

TAKE CONTROL WITH ACTION

My first year with Roger Penske was in 1979. This was also the first year of the ground-effects cars. Colin Chapman, of Lotus, was way ahead of the rest of the world in racing car design. He was a pioneer who looked at things other than horsepower to make a car go faster through turns and use aerodynamics to enhance the car's performance. One of the other things he figured out was how to use the air rushing under the car to his advantage. Without getting into the engineering details, Colin found out that he could create a vacuum under the car by modifying how air flowed underneath it. This he called ground effects. By understanding how this vacuum worked, car designers could take advantage of actually sucking the car to the ground, getting much better cornering speeds. In racing, the ground-effects cars were secret aerodynamic developments that were really increasing the speeds by using a force that was basically free—no aerodynamic drag, but more down force. Penske invested a lot of money over the winter to develop the new ground-effects car, his model PC-7. The year before, his team had been running PC-6 cars, but the PC-7 was really the one that was the future for me and Roger.

I ran a race in April at Atlanta that year, which was held before the Indy 500. We didn't do as well as expected; the car simply wasn't fast enough. We were just getting to understand how the ground effects worked on the car, but weren't totally certain on what adjustments we needed to make to get more speed.

After the race, Roger and I were talking about what to do for Indianapolis. Roger said, "I've already called England (where Penske's cars were being built) and have ordered two new PC-6s (Penske Car model number 6, which was the previous year's model) for you and Rick (my teammate, Rick Mears) with all the stuff you've developed for the PC-7 that we know is better."

"Rog, go ahead and get one for Rick, but don't get one for me, because I think the PC-7 is going to be faster in time. I just need a few more breakthroughs and I think I'll find them pretty soon."

He just looked at me and said, "Are you sure that's what you want?"

"Yep. I think we're real close to a major breakthrough on the PC-7. I just need a little more time."

Roger was against this because he was going to shelve the PC-7 development until later that year and just focus on racing the PC-6s. I told him, "Let me do one more test. I have a good idea what might work, but I need to test it. Then if it doesn't work out, you can put the car upstairs (retire it)."

"Well all right. Where do you want to do it?"

I said, "Ontario Motor Speedway in California. It's the smoothest and has the least amount of wind so we can really run some good tests. I really need one good day."

"Bobby, we've got to be in Indianapolis next week! We've got to make a decision *now*, because I've got a factory in England putting together two cars for you and Rick Mears and we're going to fly them over to Indy next weekend."

Roger and I started figuring the schedule and logistics to get the test done in California and still have cars ready to go in Indianapolis by next weekend. We figured out there simply wasn't enough time to do this. But Roger didn't give up, even though he wasn't so sure about doing this test. He started to think decisively how to do this. He asked me if I knew if Ontario was available. I said I didn't, so we walked over to the pay phone—there were no cell phones back then—and Roger plugged a few coins in and dialed the Ontario Speedway. It turns out that the track was taken.

We found out that Ontario was being used by the Champion Spark Plug Company for motorcycle testing. He asked me, "What do you think?" I had a real good relationship with Champion Spark Plugs, and had done numerous tests and ads for them for many, many years. I knew the chairman of Champion, Frank Stranahan, quite well. I told Roger that I'd guarantee we could get the track with one call from me to Champion. That was all Roger needed to know. He called Reading, Pennsylvania, and instructed his people to load a support truck with all the things they would need to run a car test and to leave for California within the hour. He then arranged to have the PC-7 car I had just driven in the race flown out to California.

In the meantime, he told his tired crew to pack up and fly to California, and be ready to test on Tuesday. Then he handed the pay phone to me and said, "Now it's up to you, Bobby. Call Champion and get the track for us."

I called Frank Stranahan at his home and asked about Ontario. He said, "Bobby, whatever you need. We're running a motorcycle test out there. They have a road course on the infield at Ontario, so when you're running your test on the big track, my people will just move to the road course until you're done. No problem."

I quickly left for Ontario. As soon as we showed up, the motorcycles moved to the infield. We only had one day to make this work. In the first hour, we made a major breakthrough. I called Penske immediately from the Ontario Speedway pay phone to let him know all of this extra effort was going to pay off. We made two more breakthroughs that day before packing up the car and air-freighting it to Indianapolis.

Through those three breakthroughs, we got a sense of direction, and were able to continue improving the handling of the PC-7 right up to the start of the 500. We didn't run fast enough in qualifying to win the pole, but after the race started, it wasn't long before people realized we had the fastest car. I led 89 laps in that race, and was leading with 20 laps to go when fourth gear went out on my transmission. The other Team Penske driver, Rick Mears, went on to win the race. The testing we had done at Ontario gave us a huge advantage in the race. This was only accomplished because of the decisiveness of Roger Penske, and because my words had real meaning with him. My ability to back up words with actions is what allowed me to take more control of my destiny. In this case, it meant running the PC-7 on my terms, not the PC-6 on Roger's.

Taking action is a significant aspect to becoming successful, but one other thing about racecar drivers having to do with words and actions is worth discussing: we don't pull any punches. Our word is our bond.

DON'T INTENTIONALLY TRIGGER FALSE ALARMS

The worst thing you can do is yell fire when there isn't one. It's one thing to bluff in a card game or in an intense negotiation, but at the end of the day, a winner's word is his bond. Racecar drivers know this. We know the importance of what we are doing, how highly dangerous our chosen profession is, and do not take any safety issue lightly.

One time my brother Al was in a race with A.J. Foyt. Al thought he saw A.J.'s rear right tire going flat, so he signaled to A.J. to pit. A.J. pitted, and it turned out to be a false alarm. However, even an extremely competitive tough competitor like A.J. Foyt knew that another driver, especially Al Unser, would have never knowingly given him a false alarm. A.J.'s pit crew wasn't as forgiving, but drivers know how serious it is when they think something is going wrong and one of their fellow drivers is in trouble. If you earn the reputation of being a man of your word, you'll be forgiven for an honest mistake.

ATTACK PROBLEMS

Nothing ever goes as planned. There's always going to be something to challenge you, and some of those challenges may be totally unexpected. That's when you have to attack it, solve it, and move on—again, you have to take action. One of the most action-orientated problems solvers I ever met was Gene McManus of the Goodyear Tire and Rubber Company. Back in Chapter 1, I talked about the problem the Unsers had running with recapped tires on the Pikes Peak Hill Climb. That was in 1958, and Firestone was not only the official tire for the Hill Climb, they had *all* racing tire business. After the race, we decided to do something about it. That's when I called the operator and asked for the Goodyear phone number in Akron, Ohio.

Here I am, calling from the sticks in Albuquerque, to a company I have never talked to before. I ask the operator to put me through to somebody in engineering that knows how to design tires. She put me through to a fellow by the name of Gene McManus.

"I'm Bobby Unser, I'm from Albuquerque, and I run the Pikes Peak Hill Climb Race. I'd like to talk to you about racing tires."

"Keep talking, we're interested," said McManus.

"I want a tire that will run on granite gravel. Are you interested in that?"

"Yes."

"Have you ever heard of walnut shells in rubber?

Long pause. "Walnut shells?"

"Yep."

"Hmmm. Let me make some samples and send them to you."

"Fine."

"Where shall I send them?"

"My garage in Albuquerque."

I had a makeshift track on my property in Albuquerque where I used to run tests on all kinds of things, including tires. So Gene McManus sent the samples to me, and I picked out the ones I wanted. He built a whole bunch of tires and sent those to me. I called him again.

"When you make the casing, do you have any choice of the way you make the casing?"

He said, "Sure."

"Can you make something other than your standard four or six ply?"

Gene answered, "Sure. What do you want, ten or twelve ply?"

"No. Can you make two-ply?"

Again, just like when I mentioned walnut shells in the first conversation, Gene was quiet for a moment. Then he said, "Two-ply?! Why do you want two-ply?"

"Because the tire is a flywheel, and I want to take weight out of it. I want to make the tires lighter. Can you make a two-ply?"

"I don't know. Wait. Yes. Sure, I can make a two-ply."

"Can you make it as strong as a four-ply?"

Gene replied, "Actually, I think I can make it stronger than a four-ply. I can give you the strength of a six-ply by just using a different nylon."

Then I asked him, "Can we get rid of the extra rubber on the side of the tires? Remember, I want to get rid of as much weight as possible."

"Sure. That's easy."

That was probably five or six phone calls, and all of a sudden I had the Goodyear factory backing me without me really knowing it. I had picked up the phone and was lucky enough to be connected to an action-oriented guy named McManus. Now with Goodyear Tire and Rubber behind us, the Hill Climb couldn't keep the Unsers out at Pikes Peak. We had a big guy with us.

I didn't know Gene McManus when I called Goodyear. I just dug up their phone number in Akron, Ohio and called them from my home in Albuquerque. Gene didn't know who Bobby Unser was, and Goodyear didn't make racing tires, but he was interested in what I had to say. He asked questions. He asked for details. He offered to send me some samples. This wasn't feigned interest. Gene McManus took the initiative to design racing tires. He didn't say it wasn't in his budget. He didn't say it wasn't his job. He saw the racing tire development as a challenge to a problem. He also realized he could solve the problem by doing something about it. Within four years Goodyear would be at the

Indianapolis 500. It wasn't long before Goodyear tires dominated the racing world.

As you can see, taking action not only helps you stay ahead of the pack, but it also helps you counterattack problems. Probably the greatest benefit from doing things is you become experienced. This experience helps you to develop a gut instinct to solve problems. The more experience you have, the more adept you become at developing smart strategies.

ACTIONS LEAD TO EXPERIENCE

In 1968, I was racing for Bob Wilke and the Leader Card Race Team. We were at Indianapolis, getting ready for the 500. We had a new Gurney Eagle from All American Racers and had won three races in a row. That wasn't good enough. We were getting close to breaking the 170 mile per hour barrier at the Indianapolis Motor Speedway. My number two mechanic—(Little Red) Tom Herrmann—and I were really determined to be the first to break 170 miles per hour.

Little Red and I were working hard on getting more speed out of the car, to the point we were getting pissed off about it. We were passionate about racing, and when you're trying to break down a barrier you are so close to, you push things a bit. We tried this adjustment and that adjustment, but just couldn't get to 170.

One day I couldn't get through the corners well. Instead of taking it back into the garage and tweaking the car, we made an adjustment right there in the pits to save time. I told Little Red, "Red, make a big adjustment. Take the right front sway anti-roll bar and run it out about three turns. Let's see what happens. I'm tired of this tweaking B.S. We've tried all kinds of springs and sway bars, and nothing is working. We've got to make a radical change."

I took the car out and there was a huge change in the handling. Big enough that I actually broke the 170 mile per hour barrier and made world news! I have no doubt that if we had made the radical change first, before making the painstakingly small adjustments, I'd have flown right into a wall. But by making the small adjustments, we learned not only how to push the envelope, but when. That's when we decided to go for it. It was a calculated risk. The experience we picked up by tak-

ing the little actions paid off handsomely when we made the more radical adjustment.

People can talk all they want about doing things, but nothing gets done until you take action. No matter how much thinking you put into anything, you don't learn anything until you actually do something. By doing something you either validate your planning and thinking, or learn to adapt. The worst thing that can happen to you by doing something is you'll learn something. With that in mind, you won't have anything to worry about by jumping in and starting your engines.

I wasn't so sure I could compete at Indianapolis—it was really hard, and the drivers were really good. When I finally took the chance and drove Andy Granatelli's Novi and qualified with the fifth fastest time among all those great racers, I knew I could compete at Indy. With each race I ran at Indy, I gained more confidence. I not only belonged in the race, but realized I could compete with the best drivers in the world.

≡ PIT STOP POINTERS

- ■ Don't be afraid to take action. You will never finish something before you start.
- ■ Challenge yourself to take action.
- ■ Punctuate your words by taking action.
- ■ Be decisive.
- ■ Don't threaten actions you can't deliver.
- ■ Aggressively attack problems to keep them from gaining control.
- ■ The more you do, the better you get.

CHAPTER FIVE

TAKING THE
CHECKERED FLAG

*T*he 1968 Indianapolis 500. The damn pin in the gear shifter had vibrated out. Not at Indy! I had Granatelli's new turbines whipped, but I couldn't use first, second, or third gear coming out of the pits. Coming out of the pits in fourth gear was costing me another half to three quarters of a lap. It killed our time, but that's what we had to deal with. The good thing was we raced 75-gallon tanks instead of the 35-gallon tanks today, so we only needed to make four refueling stops for the entire race.

Granatelli had three turbines in the race; Joe Leonard, Graham Hill, and Art Pollard. His number one driver was Leonard. With 12 laps to go, Leonard was running first, but I was 200 yards behind him and gaining ground fast. In another two laps, he was mine. Then there was an accident and the yellow caution came out. I didn't think that was a big deal either, because they'd clear up the accident in about three or four laps, and I'd take Leonard with about six laps to go.

Then another problem came up. Between Leonard and I was his teammate, Art Pollard. Pollard wasn't even in contention. Leonard and I were three laps ahead of Pollard. One of the rules under the yellow caution is that you can't gain ground on the car running in front of you. This is both for safety and to make sure nobody picks up ground under a non-race condition. One of the other rules under a caution is you can't pass anybody, and Granatelli knew this. He had Pollard's pit crew signal to Pollard to slow *down. Damn! Leonard couldn't gain ground on me, but his teammate Pol-lard could make me lose ground on Leonard by going slower. There was no rule that said Pollard had to keep pace with the leader.*

It was obvious what was happening. Even the fans knew it, and they started to rise and boo their disapproval. I pulled up next to Pollard and pointed at him to get moving. He just stared straight ahead. He knew he couldn't look me in the eye while he was doing this. Leonard's lead slowly increased with each lap. That yellow caution seemed to last forever.

Pollard had successfully dropped me back about 700 yards behind Leonard when the green flag finally came out. There were only eight laps to go. In my mind I quickly did the math: I could gain one second each lap on Leonard, roughly 100 yards. With 700 yards to pick up, I wouldn't catch him until the last lap. I would have to make my move on him on the back straight away, between turns two and three. The fans would love this, but I didn't like it at all. I didn't want to have a passing issue near the end of the race, and Joe Leonard was one reason why.

He wasn't going to let me pass in any easy way, and I damn sure wasn't going to let him stop me. Granatelli puts a lot of pressure on his drivers, and I'm sure Joe was feeling the pressure to win at all costs. This was going to be a 170 mile per hour drag race with a little bumper car action like a sprint car race. One of us, or even both of us, might get parked in the stands. . . .

L earning to finish a job makes all of the preparation, testing, planning, practicing, and effort worthwhile. It punctuates effort. There is ab-solutely no feeling that can equate to the high you get when you drive a race (or a deal) to its conclusion. I believe there are five critical aspects to becoming a consistent finisher:

1. Work with other winners
2. Eliminate excuses for failure
3. Take care of issues early
4. Take control of situations
5. Give it your all at the end

The beauty of racing Pikes Peak is that you're always faced with un-expected challenges. The road conditions constantly change and the

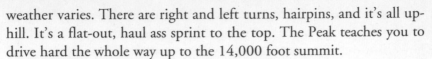

weather varies. There are right and left turns, hairpins, and it's all up-hill. It's a flat-out, haul ass sprint to the top. The Peak teaches you to drive hard the whole way up to the 14,000 foot summit.

Indy represents a different challenge. It not only tests your ability to drive at super-high speeds with 32 other hungry cats, it is a grueling road marathon that pushes your mental and physical stamina beyond any lim-its you could imagine. When I speak at corporate events, I often ask peo-ple in the audience to try to totally concentrate on one thought for as long as they can. It can be a wild fantasy, a dream, anything. The most amount of time anyone could completely focus was about three minutes. Marathon runners complete their 26 miles in a little over two hours. It takes three and a half hours to travel 500 miles at nerve-wracking speeds through 800 turns that try to pull your shoulders out of your sockets at Indy. If you want to win Indy, you have to learn to hang tough and concentrate beyond what you thought possible.

The best way to learn how to concentrate, finish, and win, is to as-sociate yourself with people who are accomplished finishers. They are usually on effective teams that have veterans with a mindset to see the total image of what it takes to drive things to a successful conclusion. Look at some of the many successful doers in business. Ray Kroc building the success of McDonald's in the '60s and '70s. Fred Smith of Federal Express continues to grow his business with a can-do phi-losophy and the people to back it up. The legacy of Herb Kelleher, founder of Southwest Airlines, continues to help that company thrive during the toughest economic times of modern air travel. All of these people succeeded by creating a finishing attitude through their own work ethic. Then they instilled that attitude in the people they hired, taught them how to eliminate excuses for failure, helped them con-front issues early on, and finally, pushed them to give their all up to the end.

BUILDING A WINNING NETWORK

Without question, working with people who are proven winners is ben-eficial to your success in anything you do. This is particularly true when it comes to accomplishing your goals. We'll talk about teamwork in much more detail in the following chapter. For now, we'll talk about how the team helps you win.

In 1966, I realized that racing for Gordon Van Liew with the Vita Fresh Orange Juice team wasn't going to make me a competitive driver at Indianapolis. Gordon was a great man, a self-made success, but there was too much turnover with his mechanics. I needed some stability with the mechanics. I wanted to go faster and finish races, not just be in them.

Quitting one team and joining another wasn't all that easy, especially if I wanted to move up to a more successful team. First of all, the other teams already had drivers. And if the drivers were successful, they were not about to get fired. Furthermore, there were probably two dozen other drivers also trying to figure out how to get on better teams. I kept looking and digging and finally found an opportunity with a team that would help me finish and win—the Leader Card Racing Team out of Milwaukee, Wisconsin.

Bob Wilke, owner of the Leader Card racing team, had already won four United States Auto Club (USAC) championships. He'd been a racing owner since the early '30s and was a proven winner. Wilke liked to run with seasoned drivers, and had 46 year-old veteran Don Branson driving for him. In 1966, most drivers were switching to the new rear-engine cars, like the Gerhardt car made in Fresno or Dan Gurney's Eagles. Don Branson didn't like the rear-engine cars, and insisted on staying with the front-engine roadsters. However, owner Bob Wilke and veteran chief mechanic Jud Phillips wanted to go with the new technology, which meant a rear-engine car. The timing was right: I was looking for a new team to help me finish and Bob Wilke was looking for an experienced driver who wanted to drive a new rear-engine car for him.

Wilke wouldn't just dump a great veteran driver like Branson. He wasn't that kind of person. There was a second Leader Card team, run by chief mechanic A.J. Watson, and Wilke hooked me up with Watson's team. The problem with Watson was that the fire in his belly was gone and he was happy to finish third or fourth in a race. He was cruis-

ing toward retirement. I wanted to finish *first*. Wilke's real plan was to park me temporarily with Watson until he could figure out what Branson was going to do.

Luckily for me, Don Branson could see the writing on the wall and he decided to retire. As soon as he quit, Bob Wilke gave me Branson's ride on Jud Phillips' team. Finally I was with a super team that wanted to do things right. Jud Phillips and Little Red Herrmann had a reputation for building cars that could finish races and go fast. I figured if Jud and I could work together to build a car that would help me go fast *and* finish, we were going to win some races.

I couldn't have hit the pay-dirt any better than when I signed with Wilke and Jud Phillips. Both were veterans who still had the desire to win, just as I did. This team had an added bonus—number two mechanic Tom "Little Red" Herrmann was as good as they ever got. We really had something going.

We started making changes right away. First, Jud bought a new rear-engine car. He got one from Gerhardt out of Fresno, California. I didn't like the Gerhardt at first, but after a while, we started to be a little more competitive. Still, we could only manage a fourth place finish at best. The beauty of working with Jud was he combined his conservativeness in building a car to finish the race with his willingness to try new technologies.

Finally, in 1967, Wilke, Jud, Little Red, and myself decided to buy an Eagle from Dan Gurney. We started 1968 with four straight wins, including the Indy 500. We worked and worked and worked, and made it to the top because we all wanted the same thing—to win. Remember how mad Little Red and I became when we were trying to break the 170 miles per hour barrier at Indy in May of 1968? That collective desire-to-win attitude is what got us there.

When I think about businesses that really know how to finish, I look at the parcel package shippers. United Parcel Service and Federal Express are the two preeminent players. Do you ever think about whether or not your package will be delivered by these companies? As big as they are, they have developed a reputation for finishing the job and delivering what they promise, no matter where or how.

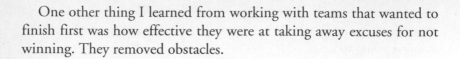

One other thing I learned from working with teams that wanted to finish first was how effective they were at taking away excuses for not winning. They removed obstacles.

TAKE AWAY EXCUSES

Roger Penske's theory of operation was, if you eliminate all reasons to lose, you'll increase your chances to win. I've adopted that theory, and suggest you do as well. In 1980, we were developing the PC-8 (Penske Car Eighth Configuration) for Team Penske. It was May, and we were at Indianapolis getting ready for the 500. I knew we needed a new wing for the car, but the problem was it took two to three weeks to fabricate a wing after being designed. I went up to Roger and said, "Roger, I need a new rear wing on this PC-8."

Penske said, "Well, let's build it."

"The problem, Rog, is I know what I want, but we don't have time to build it."

He said, "Why?"

"Because we have to get everything done to make it—drawn up, built, and back here for me to test. We don't have that many days left."

Roger pulled out a piece of paper and a pencil and said, "Draw what you want this wing to look like."

I made the little drawing and he took it. Then he grabbed his fabricator, Jerry Breon, and gave him the drawing. Jerry was one of the best and fastest fabricators in the world. He sent Breon with the drawing back to the shop in Reading, Pennsylvania, on his Learjet. Within two hours of our conversation, Roger had Jerry building the wing. As soon as Breon was done, he flew back in the Learjet that had waited for him. Within 24 hours, instead of three weeks, I was testing a new wing on the PC-8 at Indianapolis. Roger Penske eliminated all excuses. The payoff came when we qualified the car on the outside of the front for the race.

Another way to eliminate excuses is to plan for them. By 1981, drivers and pit crews were all using radios. They were electronic, and with all of the intense vibration caused by the engine, they often failed. The failure rate was something like 50 percent, which was totally unacceptable. Roger was tired of the failures, so he called the chairman of Motorola and asked him to send some engineers down to Indianapolis to fix my radio. We had to have the radio working for the race, and Roger wasn't going to let a potential broken radio stand in the way of winning the Indy 500.

The engineers from Motorola flew down to Indianapolis and got the radios working. On race day, just before the race was about to start, I was sitting in my car talking to Roger Penske. We went over a few last-minute items and then he headed over to the pit area to see if we could hear each other clearly on the radio. As he got over to the pit area I pushed the button to turn on my radio. All of a sudden, smoke came pouring out of it! I had a burned up radio, and the damn race was about to start!

Fortunately, in our prerace meeting, we had planned for this occurrence. We eliminated an excuse before it became an excuse. We went back to using sign-boards to communicate while on the track. To make things simple, I fabricated a quick cheat sheet on my steering wheel. The crew would use the sign board to talk to me, and I would use hand signs to talk to them. On my steering wheel we put number "1" for tires, "2" for wing adjustment, and "3" for tire stagger. So, if I came by and flashed one finger, it meant I needed a new tire, and so on. The bottom line is, even though Roger had gone to the effort to bring in the Motorola engineers to eliminate an excuse for losing because of radios failing, even when the radios failed anyway, we negated that as an excuse as well.

Without the radio, we were at a tremendous disadvantage. For every pit stop decision that had to be made between my crew and myself, it would take at least one more lap to come in compared to the other teams who had radios. If I needed a new tire, I'd drive by and flash one finger. On the next lap the crew would put on the sign board, Right Front. I'd have to signal back with a thumb up, which meant yes, or thumb down, which meant no. If it was no, they'd have to put up another sign on the next lap until we figured out which tire I needed to change. Communicating like this could take several laps to get it right, whereas the teams with radios had instantaneous communication and could make real-time decisions.

How did we do in that race? We won. Roger Penske is the most successful car owner in the history of racing, and he does it by eliminating excuses.

Eliminating excuses wasn't the only thing that helped me win. I figured out that it was much better to race smart than it was to overpower opponents with speed alone; that's too tiring. I've got enough work just trying to drive the car fast. If I can beat someone without causing a confrontation, I'd much rather do it that way.

ATTACK CONFRONTATIONS EARLY

You don't want to have an issue late in the race. An issue in racing is when two cars are going neck-and-neck during the last laps, and somebody has to pass somebody else. This pass may very well cause an accident if things get a little too aggressive—hence, it's an issue. It's much better to win the race by outsmarting your opponents early on.

The way I took care of an issue early in the race was by breaking my opponents' spirit psychologically. If I saw somebody start to creep up on me during a race, I'd just shift into third gear and blow his doors off in a convincing way. My message to him was, "You're not going to get me today, and if you try, I've got plenty more in reserve." I broke their spirit and, in doing so, eliminated any possibility of having an issue at the end of the race.

A way to look at an issue in the business world is to not let potential problems become real problems. The sooner smaller problems are taken care of, the better. You don't want these problems to be around at the finish, because they can blow the entire deal, for sure.

Paul Page of ABC Sports was a great example of this. He was the sportscaster when I was a color commentator for ABC's Motorsports. Paul was one of the two best sportscasters I ever met (the other was Brian Williams of the CBC). There's always something going on during a telecast that causes problems with the programming, and Paul was brilliant at adapting to the situation to continue the broadcast as though nothing had happened. He told me that he had expected problems to occur, and mentally prepared to handle them.

One time we were broadcasting a race in Florida. There were maybe only four or five laps left in the race when a cloudburst hit. It rained so hard that the trailer with all the electrical equipment flooded instantly, short-circuiting the controls below and killing the electric power to the broadcast booth. The emergency generator wouldn't start, so we had no back-up power, either.

The real problem for Paul and me in the broadcast booth was our TV monitors were dead and we couldn't see what was going on in the race. We relied entirely on the monitors to broadcast the race—our booth was stuck in one turn of the racetrack, and we had no view of any other part of the track. Since the race was so close to the end, the race organizers kept it going, even though it was pouring rain.

With the ever-so-slight possibility that our voice out-feed from our booth was still working, Paul kept on broadcasting the race. He did it just in case the TV audience could hear him, not knowing at all (the power in to our headsets was dead, too) if indeed his audio was going out. What amazed me was he was doing this without the benefit of the monitors, without the benefit of any audio input to his headset, and only seeing a small fraction of the racecourse. To top that off, the cars that did come by were really obscured by all the water they were spraying.

It turns out that the audio out-feed from our booth *was* the only thing that was working. What's even more amazing is Paul was so controlled and did such a good job broadcasting, that the television audience never picked up on the fact he was calling the race "blind." That's what thinking about problems and solving them before they become a crisis does for you. Just the *habit* of preparing and adapting can help you even if you don't prepare specifically for what occurs.

LEAD TO CONTROL

When you're in the lead, everyone else has to follow you. You're in control to a large degree and dictating the terms of the race, so it becomes easier. That's another reason I always wanted to lead early on: I could take care of potential issues sooner rather than later, and do so on *my* terms, not theirs.

In 1972, driving for Dan Gurney's All American Racers was a great example of taking control. Our team was constantly innovating and developing new ideas to make the Eagles go faster and faster by a wide margin. When we got to Indy that year, we absolutely destroyed the rest of the field in terms of speed. To give you an example of how much we improved car speeds, an average year-to-year increase in speed at Indianapolis was about four miles per hour. In 1972, we increased our speed by a whopping 18 miles per hour over the speed records of 1971! We accomplished more than four times the average year-to-year improvement. We had taken the lead and just knocked out the rest of the racing world with our speed. I can't even imagine how many meetings our competitors had trying to figure out what do about catching us.

All of a sudden, everybody else was scrambling to catch up to All American Racers. We totally controlled that race by leading. As mentioned earlier in the book, I had led every lap of that race for the first 32 laps, and had lapped the whole field. We did this by grabbing the lead in developing racing speed and making everyone else follow.

FINISH STRONG

"Keep driving!" Dan Gurney radioed to me in the 1975 Indy 500. I was in the lead with 27 laps to go, just ahead of Johnny Rutherford. A cloudburst came out of nowhere and dumped huge raindrops, flooding the track instantly. Leading near the end of the race—nothing was going to take that from us now—especially not the weather. I kept plowing through the water, following A.J. Foyt's orange car as it faded in and out of the terrible mist ahead of me. Finally, the red flag came out, the race was halted, and I had won my second Indianapolis 500!

Staying focused despite the sudden cloudburst (there were raindrops about half to three-fourths of an inch in diameter just pounding down out of the sky) was the key to winning the 1975 Indy 500. It was actually a lesson I learned the hard way in the 1969 Indy 500. I was running third in '69, behind Dan Gurney, who was still driving races then. Gurney was having some really bad problems with his car, and I was closing on him. However, by the time I would pass him, we would have already done 200 laps—the race would be over.

That was one of the most tiring Indy 500s I ever ran. We chose to drive a Lola in the '69 race instead of an Eagle, and I paid severely for it physically. Even though I was running third, I just couldn't get the car to handle right; it was a constant battle. I was blistering the right rear tire on every fuel stop. On the two hundredth lap, the checkered flag came out, and I was damn glad to see it. I pulled into the pits, and instead of hearing congratulations on fighting for third, Jud Phillips growled at me, "What'd you quit for?!"

I couldn't understand what he meant! Quit? What was he talking about?! It turns out a rule they had in that year's 500 was after the first place car took the checkered flag, the rest of the field could run another five minutes. There was another five minutes of racing left, and I surely could have beaten Dan Gurney—he was only 100 feet in front of me— and taken second in those extra five minutes! It wasn't a rules issue. I should have known the rules. I was focused on my pain, rather than re- membering the rules. Not finishing second cost our team second place and more than $20,000. I vowed to never let that happen again. That's why Dan Gurney didn't really have to remind me to keep driving in the rain in 1975, but since he knew what happened back in 1969, he thought a little reminder wouldn't hurt.

It's really hard work to put yourself in a position to win. When you've worked so hard to get to that point, why not finish the job? Pikes Peak was a great training ground for finishing strong. I had no idea how anyone else was going to do in those races, I couldn't see them. I didn't know what weather or road conditions they were going to have versus the conditions I would have. I had to go flat out the whole way, not letting up for even a split second until I was past the fin- ish line. To be a constant winner, you can't back off near the end, no matter how tired you are. Unfortunately, in 1969 I learned this the hard way, but I did learn.

There is no feeling that can describe sitting in the winner's circle at the Indianapolis Motor Speedway. You can tell long elaborate sto- ries about every victory, all the failings, the good things, the bad, and lord knows how many times I nearly died. But when it comes to the emotional rush of winning the Indy 500, I can't find the proper words to describe it.

When you work hard for something, and then finally attain that goal—finally reach the mountain top—it's the most beautiful high you could ever imagine. When I was in that victory lane at Indy in 1968, I was so high I could have driven another 500 miles right then. When I looked at the trophy and realized my name was going to be on it, I also realized there were a hell of a lot of other people who helped make that possible.

. . . I shoved the pain in my hands, arms, shoulders, and legs aside and floored it. My Eagle roared out of turn one down the front straight as though to say to me, "Let's go!" The only thing louder than my engine was the crowd. They knew what was going to happen, and 400,000 fans rose in a thunderous wave as my Eagle screamed, hunting Leonard and the turbine down on the track. The adrenaline rush exploded through my body. It wasn't going to be pretty, but I could smell victory, and the Eagle I was driving was going to win.

I couldn't find Leonard. Where was he? He couldn't have been that far ahead! As I came around turn four I saw my number two mechanic "Little Red" Herrmann hold out the sign board that I'll never forget: "ANDY OUT." I couldn't believe it! All of Andy Granatelli's turbines, including Joe Leonard's, were out of the race! It turned out that as soon as the green flag came out at the end of the yellow caution, Joe Leonard floored his turbine and it flamed out. He had a broken fuel pump. Now I was in the lead!

Just seven laps to go! I couldn't make any mistakes—the race was mine to lose, and I wasn't about to do that. I followed Dan Gurney, staying in his tracks, just to make sure no debris would take me out. I let him do my street sweeping for me. Those were the longest laps I ever ran at Indy.

With each lap, the crowd got louder. It was unbelievable. On the final lap, they were all waving. I came out of turn four through the front straight and down into turn one. The Eagle cruised out of turn two into the back straight on to turn three. As I approached turn four, my excitement was greater than I could even imagine. I couldn't wait to see the view coming out of turn four. As I came out of turn four, I saw a visual that was the greatest thing I have ever seen: Pat Vidan waving the checkered flag for me at the Indianapolis 500!

≡ *PIT STOP POINTERS*

- Work your way onto a winning team.
- Remove excuses to not win.
- Take care of issues before they become problems.
- Lead to control.
- Finish strong.

CHAPTER SIX

RACES ARE WON IN THE PITS

DAN GURNEY'S ALL AMERICAN RACERS—THE POWER TEAM

You know you're on the right racing team when the owner, Ozzie Olson, has a 100 foot yacht because "fishing's too slow." Olson, president of Olsonite, worked hard and played harder. He was the owner I drove for in the '70s. Ozzie funded the race entry fees and the car costs for the Gurney Eagle I drove that was built and run by Dan Gurney's All American Racers. What a team we had—Lots of power and super handling in those cars!

Dan Gurney, owner All American Racers, Anaheim, California: former race car driver (and a damn good one), and probably the best innovator in the racing business. Man, could his Eagles fly!

John Miller, engine builder from Oahu, Hawaii: John built "King Kong" power into his engines. He was light years ahead of everyone else in engine design and development. In fact, his entire focus was power, which meant his engines ran real fast. He produced so much power out of 158 cubic inches that we would get more than 1100 horsepower. Then the problem was figuring out how to get the engine to finish a race under the strain from John's super high-power designs.

Wayne Leary, mechanic, Arizona: Wayne joined Dan Gurney's All American Racers in 1966 and was instrumental in keeping the Eagles

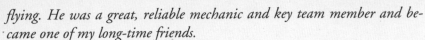
flying. He was a great, reliable mechanic and key team member and be-came one of my long-time friends.

Phil Remington, *fabricator: Phil could build a car out of a piece of tin foil. He was the best in the business in those days and still is today. He made our Eagles look like they were going 200 miles per hour when they were parked in the garage.*

In 1971 and 1972, with this team, we won 15 out of 21 poles! That's serious performance! And that's what serious teamwork is all about.

I was a successful racecar driver. That is what I did. I enjoyed doing it and excelled in doing it. But I learned early in my career that a driver was just one part of the team that was winning a race. There were many other people I had to rely on to be successful. Thus, understanding how to assemble a team became as important as learning how to set up a car. If you want to be a success at anything you do, whether it be president of a corporation, a senior executive, a manager, or administrative assistant, you have to realize more than anything else that you're going to need a supportive team. Understanding what type of team you need, what role each member of the team plays, and finally how to assemble and motivate these people is vital to achieving sustained success.

WHO ARE YOUR TEAMMATES?

At 220 miles per hour, there's no such thing as a small job. If one adjustment is not right, one detail left undone, the car could hit a wall, crash, and erupt into a ball of flame. There may be one person driving the car, but there are a lot of people who make a car go fast, keep it together, and help make it win. Putting together the *right* team—pit crews, mechanics, sponsors, and engineers—takes a long time. Egos often get in the way. Through it all though, by focusing on doing things the right way you develop a crew that thinks and acts like a real team. In my view, there are six components to a successful team, racing or otherwise, and the racing jargon becomes but a metaphor for business at large. They are:

1. Driver
2. Mentors
3. Sponsors
4. Owners
5. Crew chief
6. Pit crew

Driver

The driver is the person behind the wheel—the person with the ultimate responsibility during a race. The driver is *you*. No one else's foot can be on the gas pedal during a race but yours. As a result, it's imperative to remember that as you develop your team you must remain at the center of the universe as it relates to your goals, objectives, and responsibilities. This is not an ego thing—it's the reality of having responsibility. Everything you do in setting up your team for success must be relative to what you want to accomplish. After all, the only person who really cares about your career or your responsibilities is you. Life is your ride, not anyone else's. You can make the most of it by taking control.

It's critical to realize that people may play multiple roles on your team. For example, my agent and business partner of more than 35 years, Bruce Barnes, has been at times a mentor, at times a "crew chief," and at times an "owner" and most importantly, a close friend. One of the things I admire most in Bruce is his ability to communicate effectively. He knows how to phrase things so they are clearly understood by anyone he is addressing. That's probably why he's the best agent in the racing business. Roger Penske has been a great owner and a mentor. Without question, he is the best racing executive I have ever worked for. Roger gave me the opportunity to prove my ideas, as he did with many of his people. He didn't just give you a blank check. He listened, asked some questions, and then gave you the opportunity to succeed. Those people that were successful with their ideas continued to get the opportunities. I was fortunate enough to have more successful ideas than failures—a success rate over 60 percent, according to Roger, so he gave me plenty of opportunities. When you look at the various components of your team, keep in mind that there may be several people who can play any one role, and any one person may be able to play multiple roles.

Where do you start building your team for success? Who do you look to first? For me, I looked to a few mentors for start-up guidance.

Mentors

In the beginning of your quest for success, good guidance is the best way for you to learn before you get experience. Many corporations seek varying experiences when they assemble their boards of directors. Why reinvent the wheel when you can learn from others who not only went through trials and tribulations, but applied the lessons of their experiences?

My daddy was my first influential mentor. In Chapter 1, I explained how his can-do entrepreneurial spirit instilled in me the attitude that no matter what the challenge, there was a way to meet it. A real true mentor from the racing world who helped me get into the Indy 500 was none other than the great Parnelli Jones. Parnelli was the one who saw my talent as a driver, which proved significant because I never thought of myself as a great driver. Actually, I never realized that I was all that talented of a driver until I retired. Having a great driver like Parnelli believing in me was incredibly helpful, particularly at Indy.

Some mentors stick with you for the long haul, like my daddy and Bruce Barnes, others are only there for a moment, like Lloyd Axle. Lloyd Axle was a great midget car race driver from Denver in the 1940s and 1950s. You'll see in Chapter 9 that I talk in more detail about how he helped me cope with a terrible tragedy in the Mexican Road Race. In that instance, Lloyd was there for only a moment, but his brief guidance had profound impact on the rest of my racing career. Regardless of how long mentors are around, it's important to have them in your career. They can see your talent even if you don't see it. They can also use their wisdom to guide you through the fog of inexperience.

There is no one way to find a mentor. However, if your level of desire to excel is high enough, and you put passion and energy into what you do, invariably mentors will find you. It goes back to my mantra of "go fast, lead, win." By doing so you will catch people's attention. My relationship with Parnelli evolved mainly because I demonstrated the ability I had to go fast.

Sponsors

Early in my career, I realized if I was going to be competitive, I'd have to use someone else's money to do it. The winnings at the many super-modified races weren't going to help me build faster cars. They barely paid our basic expenses, and with a wife and two kids, I had some people depending on me to make some money. I had to find a sponsor to pay for my front-end expenses.

Whether you need financial resources to get an education (scholarship), a new piece of equipment (bank loan), or a way to fund your first business (an investor), you need to find financial resources beyond revenues or your winnings. In racing, as race teams become more competitive through their success, they have to invest more money in testing, research, and development. In business, you take a good thing and make it better. That means you need investment money *before* the next sale. You also need money to carry you through the slow times, and there are always going to be slow times. Recessions are as much a fact of business as the off-season in racing.

Good race teams continuously solicit sponsors, even when they don't need their financial support, because they just never know who will say "yes." As strange as that sounds, it's true. You never know who will say no; you never know who will say yes. Even if you don't get it by asking for it, you've planted the seeds in their minds to watch you as you grow. As you succeed, they'll more than likely invest later on. People like to invest in winners. Time and again, you'll hear savvy investors say they don't invest in companies, they invest in people. Therefore, the key to attracting sponsors is to prove your mettle as a bankable person.

The first car owner I drove for whose last name wasn't Unser was Dick Hall. He paid me $500 a month to build and race a Pontiac stock car in the United States Auto Club circuit for him in 1958. However, even the money from Dick Hall wasn't going to be enough to finance the family and help build my racing career. I put feelers out to look for more car owners. Bud Trainor, a racing friend from Phoenix, hooked me up with the fastest sprint car in the Southwest—the ECCA (Elloy Cotton Chemical Association). The problem was the owner, Kirk Purvis, was going broke. I had to come up with $100 of my own money to run in my first sprint car race. Still it was one of the best deals I ever made. Instead of a sponsorship, which was what I was looking for, I ended up gaining renown as a competitive car winner throughout the racing business. It would bring me a lot of attention from many sponsors.

In my first race, I wound up second out of 40 cars, barely losing after running out of fuel. First place went to Bud Sterrett. Sterrett's owner, Les King, was so impressed with my driving that he hired me to drive for him after that race. I had jumped from someone who was broke and required his driver to bring in money to someone who actually could afford the car *and* the driver. The ECCA car did what I wanted it to do: it got me some attention from reputable owners.

Again, it's all about going fast, leading, and then possibly winning. You need to lead races not just to be competitive. You want to set an example as an exciting race driver and potential winner. In business, the more ways you can demonstrate your mettle, savvy, or what-have-you, the more attention you will start to attract. You never know who's watching.

Fans (customers) are what really fuels the team with funds, but car owners are the ones who prime the pump. In the early stages of racing, the owner and the sponsor may be one in the same. As the success grows, so does notoriety, and the stakes get bigger. It gets to a point where the owner can no longer finance the operation alone. Additional sponsors have to be brought in. Like an owner, they take a risk, but it's a calculated risk. In our business, the sponsors loved racing and the attention it brought to their products. They knew they'd get great exposure to fans, which would translate into increased sales.

In business, whether it's your bank, friends and family, or stockholders, you need that extra supply of money to help you grow. Some race team owners had a hard time soliciting and bringing in outside money because they didn't like to give up any control. Just as the racing world changes, so does the business world. You have to face the fact

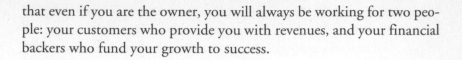
that even if you are the owner, you will always be working for two people: your customers who provide you with revenues, and your financial backers who fund your growth to success.

Owners

Every enterprise, whether it be large or small, needs someone who can look at the big picture and make smart decisions on how to leverage resources—money, equipment, and personnel. For a one-person show or your own career, this typically is yourself or a mentor. For small businesses, it may also be a hired consultant. For a large business, the job and title become a full-time position: chief executive officer.

> *Owners are owners for a reason. They know how to negotiate. When Parnelli Jones found out I was going to drive for Andy Granatelli, he told me to make sure I didn't drive for less than a $10,000 fee. With this good piece of advice from Parnelli, I marched down to Granatelli to negotiate my driving fee. I marched out with $1500. I was a pushover. Where was Bruce Barnes when I needed him?*

In the racing business, the team owner is the person who provides you your "ride." This is the businessman in racing who puts it all together: the CEO of a race team. The owner controls the money. We may drive for the fans, but we work for the owners. At the end of the race, they are the ones who divvy up the spoils and write the checks to the team. The best owners are the ones who know how to be decisive and take charge, a benevolent dictator.

On the other hand, you have CART—the Championship Auto Racing Teams—as a prime example of what I believe is inefficient leadership. It is currently made up of 19 race teams that meet and make all of their decisions. As you may know, they're getting their lunch eaten by

NASCAR because NASCAR is run by a benevolent dictator—a good one, mind you—named Bill France, Jr., and CART is run by a bunch of people who can't agree on much of anything. CART is in so much trouble today because they can't make a decision that works for everyone. As a result of constant political in-fighting, CART suffers.

However, CART has recently made a significant change by putting Chris Pook in charge. If the teams let Chris run the show, then there's hope. If they don't, they'll have the same old problems.

My first owner technically was my father. He gave me my first ride. After that, I had to scrap and scrape to build my own car. Then Dick Hall paid me to drive his Pontiac in 1958. He was a wealthy sportsman who had enjoyed watching me race super-modifieds. Remember what I said about "You never know who's watching"? That's why you lead as often as you can. Somebody watching you might be the golden ticket to help your business grow.

My first CEO for the 1963 Indy 500 was John Chalik. John saw me win numerous races in the ECCA car in 1962. He knew I had multiple victories as well as record times in the Pikes Peak Hill Climb. Those wins and Parnelli Jones supporting me convinced him that I could drive his Offy roadster at Indy. However, when John stopped funding my practicing before the 1963 Indy 500, I had to find another CEO fast, or I wasn't going to be in that race.

Fortunately, my daddy championed my cause by pestering Parnelli Jones into pursuing Andy Granatelli, who owned several powerful Novi cars. As I mentioned earlier, Parnelli won the pole for that Indy 500 by shattering the 150 mph barrier with a qualifying speed record of over 151 miles per hour. I ran the Novi at 147 miles per hour and eventually turned in a 149 mile per hour qualifying time. That definitely put me on the radar screen for other owners at Indy.

Adapt or Quit: The Cost of Success for the CEO

In the late 1960s, with the introduction of turbines, aerodynamics, fuel developments, and tire testing, the cost to compete just became too great for any one owner. Other sources of money had to be brought in to develop newer and faster cars. That's when race teams really evolved: Granatelli, Parnelli Jones, Dan Gurney, and Roger Penske. They moved racing into a full-blown business enterprise. As an owner, you had to get on board with the change or bail out before you went bankrupt.

In 1968, owner Bob Wilke did a great job helping our team become successful. We won the Indy 500 and the USAC Championship. However, by 1970, our success had outgrown Wilke's ability to fund it. He couldn't afford a winning team anymore. Bob was a great person and one of the greatest owners ever, but he had no desire to go beyond his own financial resources to fund a racing team in a changing business. By 1970, the cost of maintaining a competitive race team drove him out of racing altogether.

Just as the cars I drove have evolved, so had the business world. I worked for Dennis Lewin, Senior Vice President of Sports Production, when I was a color racing analyst at ABC Sports. After working at ABC, Dennis moved to the National Football League as the Senior Vice President in charge of Communications (radio and television contracts). Dennis told me how the NFL became even more successful when its family-style culture under the strong leadership of Commissioner Pete Rozelle, evolved into a newer, more business-style culture under Paul Tagliabue. Tagliabue became the Commissioner of the NFL in 1989, and has master-minded its continued successful growth at a time when other professional sports leagues seem to be faltering.

CEOs in business are the same as racecar owners. Just as racing has changed, business owners also need to adapt to stay successful. They have to see that things change as a business matures. If the owners adapt with the business, and they involve themselves with the change that goes on around them, they will, more likely than not, remain successful. As you examine your own situation, if you find yourself in a position in which your boss is not going to provide you with, say, the latest technology that will help you become more successful, perhaps it's time to look at other opportunities—just as I had to leave Bob Wilke.

Crew Chief

The crew chief is the one who keeps everything running smoothly. Jud Phillips was the first great chief mechanic I worked with. Jud and I hooked up when I moved to Bob Wilke's Rislone Sponsored/Leader

Card Race Team in mid-1966. He was a seasoned veteran, and smart enough to keep up with the changing times. He was one of the first chief mechanics to push changing to the rear-engine cars. The first rear-engine car I had was a Gerhardt, which wasn't the fastest, but Jud really knew how to get the most out of it. In 1967, we bought one of Dan Gurney's new Eagle Offy powered cars. That really made us a fully competitive team: driver, owner, mechanic, and car.

Jud had a great assistant, Tom Herrmann. Little Red was short and really strong, and had a habit of putting away lots of beer after working hours. With Little Red, work was work, and play was play. In 1968, this team—Bob Wilke, owner; Jud Phillips, chief mechanic; Little Red Herrmann, assistant mechanic; and myself driving—won five races including the Indy 500, and finished 14 races fifth or better. We won the USAC National Driving Championship that year. When you have a good team, good things will most always happen.

The same is true for every company that is successful: it's not just the CEO, or the Vice President of sales. It's *all* of the management working together toward a common objective. They all must have the desire for the same things.

Pit Crew

In today's technology-driven world, taking care of details is vital, just like it is in auto racing. One wrong adjustment, one missing part, one piece of incorrect data, and a whole system can be shut down. Not only is it necessary to get the details right, but with a good team, getting the details right and doing them quickly can gain a significant advantage in the time department.

Roger Penske figured it out in the early 1970s: pit time was wasted time. If he could get his systems and his people to reduce the time his cars spent in the pits, he would gain "soft" driving time on the track. Pit crew people have defined roles. They practice their role, over and over again. They need to combine athletic skill with mechanical capability in a pressure-packed environment. Not much room for lost time, no room for errors.

Roger Penske's teams have a reputation for the fastest pit times. They have won numerous awards, including the Indy 500 Pit Crew contest many times, which is held a couple of days before the Indy 500. Our race team with Penske still holds the Indy 500 track record for a fueling and tire change pit stop of eight seconds. To put this in perspective, it takes ten seconds for a telephone to ring three times. Penske's pit crew provided a car with approximately 35 gallons of fuel and changed all four tires in the same amount of time you would expect a good business to answer its customer service line—in less than three rings.

While your support staff may not directly be revenue generating, avoid the common mistake of viewing them purely as an expense item. Everybody's a producer on the team. A properly trained and motivated support staff can gain you a considerable amount of "soft driving time."

Assembling and Working with Your Team

It is always challenging to assemble a good team, but it's not impossible. You have to find good people, and if you're an unknown, it's all the more difficult. Most of the good people are already taken by someone else. Sometimes, you have to make people good. We'll talk about that later when we talk about accountability and responsibility. However, even with good people, circumstances occur in which they will be available. For example, their employer may have moved out of town or gone out of business. Recessions are great times to find good talent. Or, maybe someone is just tired of working for a certain company and needs to work in a new and more challenging environment.

There are four overall traits I look for in people I consider hiring. The first two traits are the ability to show up on time, and the desire to take initiative to do something—not just pass time. It sounds simple, but you'd be surprised. If someone can't show up on time and if he doesn't have the right attitude, you don't need him. Next, he has to be trustworthy. You can't have someone stealing from the company, or cheating on what he does. Finally, he has to be able to do the job. Thus, you need people who:

- Show up on time
- Try
- Are honest
- Do their job well

This is a tall order to fill. But given the importance of the team and the role they'll play in your ultimate success, it's worth the effort to recruit the right people. Sometimes you have to dig hard to find them, but if you dig in the right spots, you'll have much better luck.

Where Do You Find Good People?

If you know where to look, you can reduce the time it takes to find good people. For me, the first place I always looked was to my family and friends. My dad was a good mentor and mechanic, and my brothers Jerry, Louis, and Al helped with building and testing cars. Mom kept the books and managed the office. Charlie Berger used to help me often in my early racing career. Charlie was a good friend in Albuquerque who loved cars as much as I did. He helped out at Daddy's garage and was a part of the family. I was really fortunate to have such a hard-working family and good close friends at the start of my career.

If the family and friends route isn't available, you have to broaden your search. At one end of the age spectrum you have young people who are eager to start. Once at Indianapolis, there was a young kid named Randy standing by the fence near the garage. Every day he kept calling me over to the fence, "Mr. Unser! I'd really like to work on your race team." We always had people asking us if they could work on our crew, and we were pretty well set in the team we had. Randy was different. You could see it in his eyes and hear it in his voice. He had the desire to do this, and really wanted to be on our team.

I went over to our crew chief, Jud Phillips, and told him I wish he would take a look at this kid. Jud just growled, "I don't need anybody now!" Randy didn't give up, and Little Red and I kept after Jud. The difference between Randy and any others asking to be on our crew was Randy wanted to help us, the others wanted to help themselves. They were in it more for the notoriety, to brag to their friends that they were on Bobby Unser's crew. Not Randy. He didn't just want to work on Bobby Unser's crew; he really wanted to help. Jud finally took him on to our crew and Randy stayed with us for many years.

Just as Randy represented youth on the rise, so did Jud Phillips represent a veteran not quite ready to retire. Even if someone has retired,

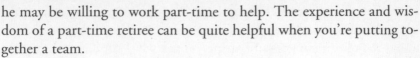

he may be willing to work part-time to help. The experience and wisdom of a part-time retiree can be quite helpful when you're putting together a team.

The military is another good source of employees. They have the experience of working in a team environment, and skills training to go along with it. Many people in the military are given significant responsibilities. There are 24-year-olds in the United States Air Force flying $236 million C-17s into war zones. These people understand the significance of accountability and teamwork. We had many terrific mechanics, like Wayne Leary, who came out of the service.

Credentials and character

It may sound strange to hear "credentials and character" uttered in the same breath. But, actually, they are two sides of the same coin. On one hand, you can't afford to be fooled by credentials because they're just pieces of paper. How someone performs with the credentials he has earned is what matters. On the other hand, character only goes so far as well. I'm not going to hire somebody to work on my car if he doesn't know anything whatsoever about race cars, no matter how good his character is. Likewise, I won't hire somebody who has great credentials, but can't make it to work, isn't a team player, or is dishonest. Credentials and character go hand in hand.

An example I had of a great team in the business world was when I went to work for the Canadian Broadcasting Company (CBC). Doug Sellars was the first person I worked with at CBC, and a key to me doing the two Canadian Indy Car Race broadcasts for CBC each year. There were others at CBC that made the CBC experience great as well. Larry Kimber followed Doug at CBC, and was a tremendous leader for the Indy Car Race broadcast team.

Brian Williams was my partner in the broadcast booth, and what a great person he was. He was always having a good time, and just a completely positive person. You could throw Brian Williams out of an airplane and he'd talk all the way to the ground and make you feel good about the trip down!

There was no government intervention at CBC, even though it was a government-run company. The company treated me like family. The people working at CBC were not cutthroat as is often the case in the United States broadcasting business. If I screwed up, they teased me about it rather than get mad at me. That's what families do: they are supportive, not antagonistic. (I'll talk more about family in The Family Wildcard, Chapter 12.) The fans loved us, too. We just blew the ratings out of the roof compared to competitive broadcasts.

One time a driver got killed in a race we were covering. The folks at CBC had never had that happen before. Nobody from the television production truck up to the broadcast booth knew what to do. But I knew what to do, so they turned to me and let me run the show. No questioning. There was no posturing about who was in charge. There was just instantaneous teamwork following my lead and we all did a great job. They were really good people to work with.

When You Don't Pick the Team: Playing the Hand You're Dealt

It's nice to build the right team from scratch, but you may not be in that position. In my early racing days at Indianapolis and other places, I didn't have a choice of mechanics. I had to take who I was given and make the best of it. When I raced for Gordon Van Liew, he had good mechanics. But his mechanics just weren't competitive enough to win. In auto racing, everyone on the team has to have that competitive chip on his shoulder. Guys like Little Red Herrmann on the Leader Card Team, and Wayne Leary from Dan Gurney's All American Racers. They wanted to do whatever it took to make my car go faster and beat the other guys.

I knew that Gordon's mechanics weren't going to help make us a competitive team. Gordon was the boss, and these were his people, so I had to make the most of it, and I did. I just worked a little extra harder trying to convince the team to do a few more things with the car setups than they were inclined to do. It's hard when you're used to doing everything yourself, and your standards are so much higher than the person you are working for. You have to try to get more out of the people than they normally produce, without getting them or the owner too bent out of shape. You need to rock the boat without tipping it over.

We did pretty good with the Vita Fresh Orange Juice teams from

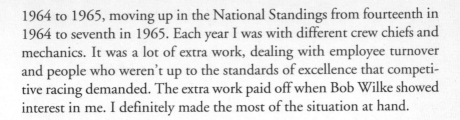

1964 to 1965, moving up in the National Standings from fourteenth in 1964 to seventh in 1965. Each year I was with different crew chiefs and mechanics. It was a lot of extra work, dealing with employee turnover and people who weren't up to the standards of excellence that competitive racing demanded. The extra work paid off when Bob Wilke showed interest in me. I definitely made the most of the situation at hand.

Training

Education is so important to any individual or any group's success, that I've devoted a whole chapter to it later in the book, Education: The Ultimate Performance Enhancer. However, I need to mention education as a means of developing a successful team now, while we're talking about building the team.

Training gets a team to do the right things in the right order, like Penske's pit crew was noted for doing. You also need to prepare them for the events that are most likely to go wrong, much like a fire drill. Knowing who does what when something goes wrong is great training in handling crisis situations. By giving positive order to a bad situation, you put the team in a proactive mode to react to a crisis. You'll find that in crisis situations, when people are properly trained and prepared for them, they will respond with incredible vigor. Look at the Coalition Forces in the Gulf War. They were not only trained for combat, they trained for four months specifically for Operation Desert Storm. Combat, by its very nature, is a crisis-laden environment. The test of true teamwork comes when things go bad. Who bails out, and who stays during a crisis is the acid test for teamwork. Those who stay in the battle bond forever. Those who bail out when it's too hot are gone forever.

Communicating with Your Team

Once your team is assembled, how well you communicate with it will dictate how well it functions. Without good communication you are dead in the water. Make no mistake about it. Your communication channels need to be free-flowing, and you and your teammates need to speak in terms that can be understood by all. As I mentioned earlier, prior to on-board radios, pit crews and drivers would communicate with one another during a race by using signboards. That's even trickier than it sounds because at high speeds and the fact that you have to take your eyes off the track, pit crews could only put one or two words maximum on the board. Then, on the next lap, the driver's hand signals had to be communicated back to the pit crew quickly and clearly. At 200 mph, there was little margin for error.

Throughout the '70s, I had one guy I could really rely on for signboard communications: Bill Berkley. Bill was a Continental Airlines pilot who just loved the races and was on my crew. He could read me like a book, and that made the communications much better. His signs to me were explicit and well-written so I knew the message clearly, and he could understand my hand signals back to him. He was so invaluable to me that when I moved from Gurney's team to Fletcher's in 1977, he went with me. He was also my backup pilot for flying me home after a race in case I got hurt, which occasionally happened.

Another part of good communications is recognizing that those with whom you are dealing may not be effective communicators. Asking questions thus becomes of paramount importance. Intentional or not, what people say and what they mean to be saying are often two different things. During my life, I noticed that some of best "bad communicators" have been in the racing business.

Look what happened when drivers didn't ask questions before the Texas Firestone Firehawk 600 race in 2001. The Texas Motor Speedway has 24 degree banked turns that are higher than the 18 degree banked turns at other speedways, and subjects the drivers to much more severe G-forces in a turn. A day before the race, two drivers pulled off the track prematurely from dizziness during their practice runs. After seeing Dr. Steve Olvey, CART Director of Medical Affairs to complain about the dizziness, Dr. Olvey took it upon himself to call a meeting and ask all 24 drivers if they had experienced dizziness. They all raised their hands! Then they proceeded to talk about how they had never experienced such G-forces and dizziness anywhere else. Ultimately, the race was cancelled. Why hadn't someone brought this up sooner? I guess they didn't want to look like a bunch of sissies.

Meetings

A natural outgrowth of teamwork and communications are meetings. Meetings with solid, relevant agendas can be quite useful (e.g., prerace driver meetings). On the other hand, meetings used improperly can be an enormous waste of time. When I was providing color commentary for ABC Sports, we used to have countless meetings before broadcasting a race. We'd talk about everything at these meetings, *except* matters pertaining to the broadcast team. For example, my colleagues spent countless hours discussing where the cameras were going to be positioned. That just wasn't pertinent information for a meeting with the broadcast team. The camera people knew what they are doing. We were broadcasters, not cameramen.

What we needed to talk about at our meetings was how to get more people to watch the race. What could we do this race that would make it more interesting to the viewers so they would tell their friends? That would have been a fruitful meeting.

As much as I talk here about the meetings at ABC that drove me crazy, let me also add that that was the *only* thing I didn't like about working for ABC. Overall, ABC was great to me. They gave me a great opportunity to broadcast with a great broadcast team, and it started from the top with Dennis Swanson. Dennis was the Vice President of ABC Sports when I was a color commentator. I'll talk more about Dennis later in the book. Paul Page, I already mentioned, was one of the best sportscasters I ever worked with. Bob Goodrich, who was the program producer and ran all those meetings, did a fabulous job producing motor sports. He was an incredibly smart person—he could remember everything, even when there was a lot of commotion going on. There were some really good people at ABC that I thoroughly enjoyed working with.

When I was a color analyst for CBC, there were two reasons I really liked working there. First, Doug Sellars and Larry Kimber said I could speak my mind, and I wouldn't have to worry about being politically correct. It was refreshing to work for someone who let me be me. The other reason was I didn't have to attend meetings. Doug and Larry didn't have meetings, and saw no use for them. That's probably why they

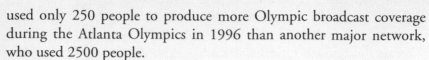

used only 250 people to produce more Olympic broadcast coverage during the Atlanta Olympics in 1996 than another major network, who used 2500 people.

If you find having meetings with your team is necessary, make sure the reasons for them are clearly understood by all, and that you stick firmly to an agenda. Nothing can pull apart team like making it feel that you are wasting its time.

Create a Sense of Urgency

One issue that frequently causes concern for many businesspeople today is the lack of passion people have for their work. Yet, there are many businesses that have proven that its employees can function in a highly motivated, highly productive environment. They're energized to perform. One way that many leaders accomplish motivating others is by creating a sense of urgency. People perform better under pressure. During a race, a pit stop is organized energy. Things have to be done quickly, correctly. No margin for error. The heightened sense of urgency makes everyone on the team perform better. A well-functioning pit crew is one of the most exciting things to watch.

Southwest Airlines has been able to create a similar sense of urgency when it turns around an airplane between an arrival and a departure. Turning a plane around—unloading an incoming flight and then re-loading the aircraft for the outbound flight—is the airline industry equivalent of a pit stop. Southwest takes 20 minutes to turn around an aircraft at the gate, which is the best in the airline industry. No other airline in the industry even comes close to that number.

This is not an easy task. A lot things have to happen simultaneously, and they have to be done right. Passengers have to get off the plane, their luggage removed, and the plane cleaned. Then the new passengers are boarded, their luggage loaded, and any new supplies such as drinks and fuel are added. All of this is done within 20 minutes.

Just as Penske realized that time in the pits during the race was wasted time, Southwest has realized that time on the ground for its air-craft is wasted time. In fact, its focus is to keep its aircraft "wheels up"—

in the air—as much as possible. The following is an example to illustrate Southwest's dedication to this effort as a team.

One month in 1983, Southwest was short on money, and needed to make payroll. The company sold one of its airplanes. But then the airline had a new problem: The company had one less plane to fly paying passengers, which meant it would make less money. That wasn't an option. The solution was to keep the same number of flights, with one less aircraft, by reducing its gate turn-around time from 20 minutes to *10* minutes—all without sacrificing safety or quality. By doing this, the airline was able to keep the same number of flights. That shows teamwork with a sense of urgency.

The end result of having a fine-tuned team, be it in racing or business, is that a good team can do things competitors can't. Every second saved in the pits is 100 yards on the track: Every extra minute a Southwest aircraft is "wheels up" is money in the company's pocket.

There may be one name on the Indianapolis 500 Winner's Trophy, but there's a whole team behind that name that made it possible. If someone says he or she accomplished something on his or her own, he's either a fool or a liar. A fool to think he did it by himself, or a liar for saying he did it by himself. Whatever your goals, there is no way you can reach them alone. You've got to realize this early on, and start to recruit your team. It's hard at first, because nobody knows who you are. But slowly, you'll find those with the desire to help with no strings attached and no preconceived notions or outcomes, just the mutual belief and recognition of desire to achieve success.

1974 National Points Champion

I won the USAC Championship in 1974 with Ozzie Olson, Dan Gurney, John Leary, Wayne Leary, Phil Remington, and the All American Racers team. In 13 Championship Races—Indy Open-Wheel races—I placed first four times; second five times; third, fourth, and fifth one time each. That's 12 top five finishes in 13 races. Now that's an ass-kicking team!

≡ *PIT STOP POINTERS*

■ Know your teammates

- Driver—that's you. You must take control of your destiny.
- Mentors—a great source of wisdom and advice.
- Sponsors—they like to invest in winners.
- Owners—the best are the those who are decisive and can take charge.
- Crew chief—the organizer who keeps everything running smoothly.
- Pit crew—the employees making sure the details are done.

■ How to make a team successful

- Look for people who show up on time, put in the effort, are honest, and do their job well.
- Make the most of what you have.
- Train your team effectively.
- Communicate openly and clearly.
- Create a sense of urgency.

CHAPTER SEVEN

TRUST AND INTEGRITY

May 16, 1968, Indianapolis Motor Speedway

*W*e did it! We broke the 170 mph barrier! I pulled into the pits and Little Red Herrmann had the biggest shit-eating grin on his face I'd ever seen. By the next day it would be world news! Everybody at the Indianapolis Motor Speedway instantly knew what had just happened, including Andy Granatelli.

Andy had three turbine-engine racecars he brought to Indy that year and he had been bragging about how they were going to blow everybody's doors off. Well, Little Red, Jud Phillips, and I just one-upped Granatelli with our Eagle.

A couple of days earlier, one of Granatelli's drivers had crashed and died. Despite this tragedy, the Indy 500 was going to be run as scheduled. Andy was looking for another driver. He swaggered over to me as I was climbing out of my number 3 Rislone/Leader Card Eagle.

He said, "Bobby, you ought to drive one of my turbines. They're the fastest cars here."

Despite the fact I had just set a new unofficial all-time record for the Indianapolis 500, I knew the turbines were more powerful. Hell, a blind man could see that.

I said, "I can't do it."

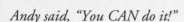

Andy said, "You CAN do it!"

"No, I can't. I've got a deal with Goodyear; I've got a deal with Bob Wilke. I've got a good team. I can't go against my word. I just won't do it."

Andy had a deal with Firestone, and these were tire-war years. Goodyear and Firestone were battling for control of Indy car racing at any cost.

He shouted, "Do you have any contracts?!"

I said, "Not with Wilke, I told him I'd race for him. We shook hands, and that's it. But I do have a contract with Goodyear. That one's in writing."

Andy said, "I'll handle the details. You just quit them and come on over here to my team. We (Firestone) will more than make up whatever you lose at Goodyear. How much do you get paid?"

I said, "Andy, how much I get paid has nothing to do with it. I made a deal with Bob Wilke and Goodyear Tire. The bottom line is that's it."

Then Andy's brother, Vince, came over and jumped into the conversation. They both started screaming at me. Andy shouted, "I don't give a damn how much they're paying you! You tell me what it is! I want to know right now! Whatever they pay you, I'll double it! How's that?!"

I replied, "Andy, you just don't understand. I have a deal with Goodyear."

Just when I finished saying that, I looked over toward the garage. Larry Trusdale, Goodyear Tire's Vice President, and Ed Alexander, the head of Goodyear Tire Development, were standing there with several other Goodyear folks. They were wondering if Granatelli was going to be successful in persuading me to switch to Firestone and his turbine with big money. I guess Granatelli's screaming started to attract attention. The people couldn't hear what was being said, but they could hear the screaming, shouting, and hand waving.

Vince Granatelli yelled, "Damn it, Bobby! Stop being so stupid! Don't you realize you are getting the best offer you're ever had?! What do you want a f—ing million dollars?! Is that what you want?! Tell me right now!"

I said, "You just don't understand. No amount of money is going to make me change my mind. That's not the issue. I have a fast car, I've got a damn good team, and I have a good deal. I'm not going back against my word. A deal is a deal, and no amount of money is going to change my mind. I wouldn't go back against my word if I had the deal with you. I'm not going against my word with Bob Wilke. So don't look for me to change.

I'm not going to do it. You and Vince can scream all you want. I'm not changing my deal with Wilke or with Goodyear."

If my daddy taught me one thing, it was to honor my commitments. He didn't tell me to do this. He didn't preach to me about it. He just did it. I never really thought that trust was something you were supposed to learn from others or would teach people about. Everybody knows what's right and what's wrong, what's good and what's bad. I never used trust as a ploy to get my way. It's just the right thing to do. It's like people asking me what it takes to be a successful driver. There's no formula; you just get up, get out, sit your butt in a racecar and drive. Then, you figure out how to make it go faster and drive some more.

What is trust? Trust is taking actions that make words believable. It's dependability, reliability, and accountability all rolled up into one. Trust is the glue that bonds people together when they're enduring tough times. It creates loyalty, integrity, and respect.

Earlier in the book, I explained how desire is the most essential ingredient within someone for success. Well, let me tell you that trust is the most important ingredient someone must have when working with others on the way to the top.

To build trust, you need to answer questions like: How do you react in a crisis? Do you give your full effort in everything you do, no matter what it is? Do your actions validate your words?

People fundamentally know that trust is a good thing. Why, then do so many good, trustworthy people sway off course? Look at all the trust problems now facing many corporate leaders. They are destroying trust in the executive ranks and faith in our markets.

A career built on trust leads to a reputation for integrity, and with that comes earned respect from your peers. Respect by your peers is an absolutely incredible rewarding career accomplishment. In today's age of material wealth and instant gratification, paving a path to success with trust, instead of greed or impatience, is more important than ever. By remembering the importance of trust, you'll not likely sway off the path when temptations come calling.

Looking back on my career, I now can fully realize what trust did for me. I'm sure you'll agree that trust will help you. While there are undoubtedly even more benefits of trust, allow me to outline three.

1. Helps ride through bumps and turns
2. Saves time from constant follow-up
3. Builds morale in teams and individuals

Helps Ride Through Bumps and Turns

In business, something is either going wrong, or it's changing. It's no different than racing. There's always some sort of pothole, bump, or debris in the road. Sometimes, there's even a major crash, creating a momentary crisis. These are unexpected events that challenge racecar drivers. In your career, there are also external events that continually affect your performance. Businesses are constantly being bought and sold, instantly changing their corporate organizational makeup. The stock market is very volatile, and international situations continue to change the business landscape.

In a race, I used my chassis set-ups to get me through the unique conditions and turns of each racetrack. When I had my chassis set-up just right, my chances of finishing in the top five of that particular race were greatly increased. A good set-up helped me run through the turns much faster.

There's a lot of insecurity in business because things change at lightning speed. In racing, just like business, things were always changing. The teams that kept up with the changes continued to win. Those that didn't got passed up. Bob Wilke couldn't adapt to the increasing costs of running a race team and got out. Don Branson didn't want to drive the new rear-engine cars and dropped Indy cars to go back to racing sprint cars. However, change isn't the cause of insecurity in the business world—it's the lack of trust in the outcome of the change.

Today, as soon as something goes wrong people worry that their division will be sold, their department budget cut, or they'll get laid off. Some people even worry when things are going right. That's how bad

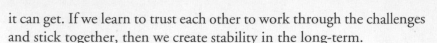
it can get. If we learn to trust each other to work through the challenges and stick together, then we create stability in the long-term.

The problem with change is people don't trust that the outcome will be better. When change occurs for the wrong reasons—like greed and impatience—then it becomes a negative thing and the result is bad. That's why people feel uncomfortable with change—anything new is presumed to be a devil they don't know. Changing for the right reasons—like improving the way things are done—is a better way to do it. Then it's not a devil of any sort. In fact, it's an angel, a savior.

When you change for the right reasons and things go wrong—and they will—people trust that the outcome will eventually improve. As long as you move ahead for the right reasons, then people won't be as stressed out about adapting; they'll feel more secure about going forward. If you are moving in a proactive, positive direction, many people will trust the change and feel secure moving forward. As much as Bob Wilke and Don Branson were not willing to change, some of the other car owners, builders, and drivers, like Dan Gurney's All American Racers were.

Trust helps you deal with unexpected crises or road debris. You have to trust yourself and your instincts to make the right decision. You also have to trust those around you, like I did my pit crew, to help you handle a crisis when things get beyond your control. A great example of this occurred in the 1995 Indy 500 when I was working the broadcast booth for ABC. Jacques Villeneuve fell way behind during the race. I can't recall everything that happened, but enough went wrong to the extent that most people would have given up. Jacques and his crew never gave up. They believed in each other and fought and fought until they won the race. Even I didn't think they had a chance to win it, but they proved me wrong.

Saves Time from Constant Follow-Up

No matter what problems I had with any racing team, owner, or anybody in business, there was one thing people knew when they dealt with Bobby Unser: I was going to show up on time and give 100 percent. If things didn't turn out in a race the way we hoped it would, it sure wasn't from a lack of total effort.

When a leader is trusted, and the leader says "Go!" his people go! The leader doesn't waste time being second-guessed by people constantly asking, "Why?" Likewise, when the leader trusts you, he or she doesn't waste time asking, "What are you doing?" "How are you going to do it?" "Why are you doing it that way?" and so on.

In Chapter 4, Start Your Engines, I recalled a time when Roger Penske and I were discussing what it would take to get more performance out of the PC-7 we used in Atlanta. We had to scramble, making several phone calls to get things in motion. Trust helped us save time in this whole transaction. We didn't have a lot of time to make a major decision, probably about one hour at the most. Roger Penske accepted that I knew what I was talking about when I said we were close to a major break-through. He had to make a major decision right then, based entirely on trust. He had a lot of money invested in the PC-7 development, but the risk of blowing Indy was huge if he decided to try my changes with the PC-7 instead of going with a sure thing, the PC-6. Without putting me through a lot of gyrations, Roger made a decision because he *trusted* me.

Then, Roger put his people in motion without hesitation. He didn't goof around. He made one call to Reading, Pennsylvania to get his people to load a truck and get it on the road to Ontario, California within the hour. Then he walked over to his tired crew at the Atlanta track and told them to pack up and head to Ontario instead of Indianapolis. Again, Roger's people trusted him and his decisions so they did not stand around and question things or drag their feet. Thus, crucial time was saved because people trusted their leader.

Trust had saved Roger and I invaluable time. Remember, Roger had already taken these actions, but we still didn't have the track in Ontario. The Champion Spark Plug Company had reserved Ontario for motorcycle testing, and it was up to me to convince their reps to let us use it. Roger Penske trusted me when I told him I could pull strings to get time on the track. I had a great working relationship with Frank Stranahan, built over many years of testing spark plugs and doing free ads for the company. When I called Frank and explained the situation, it was taken care of, in a phone call that didn't even last 15 minutes.

The time saved through trust didn't stop there. When the Team Penske entourage arrived in California and pulled into the racetrack, we didn't even have to ask the Champion people to move to the infield course to do their testing. They just moved. They trusted the instructions they were given.

It takes time to *earn* trust, but once it happens, it takes less time to manage trust. You don't have to keep checking on people to see if they're doing their job. Likewise, when you are trustworthy, others don't have to keep checking up on you. If time is money, and trust saves time, then trust saves money. It also makes money.

When I look back on my career there are a lot of people I can point to and say, "He or she helped me." Put some of them in the same room, and they might start a fight. But I could trust them and they could trust me.

When people believe in each other, they can relax about what they're doing, focus on what they need to get done, and not waste time nagging others to get their tasks done.

Builds Morale in Teams and Individuals

Another huge benefit of trust is building confidence in others by giving them the opportunity to succeed. This also builds self-confidence. People become self-assured when you give them more control over their jobs. In an Indy racecar, some drivers were given a "boost-control" and some were not. The boost control changes the turbocharger pressure, which gives you more pressure to the engine, adding more power. It's like having another gear to pass somebody. But one problem with drivers cranking the boost up too much is they burn more fuel, which results in more pit stops. The other risk is by cranking up the power, you might end up with a blown engine.

To make sure their engines didn't blow, some car builders, owners, or mechanics wouldn't give the driver a boost controller. Roger Penske trusted me, knowing that when he asked me what amount of boost I was running, he'd get an honest answer. He didn't punish me because of the mistakes of others. He gave me a controller because he knew I could be trusted to use it properly to help me win. Roger had confidence in me that I could be trusted. That was one of the reasons I enjoyed working for him. He trusted me to be accountable for my actions.

Giving people more authority to make their own decisions, like Roger Penske did, can help you when working with teams. By trusting team members to be accountable for their actions, you become a much more effective leader. You also build their self-confidence, which makes them better employees.

BUILDING TRUST

Trust is something that is earned through a combination of words and actions over a long period of time. In my career, I found three ways that trust is developed:

1. Being honest when things go wrong
2. Always giving full effort
3. Actions that back up your words

Being Honest When Things Go Wrong

In 1967, I was excited about driving for the Leader Card Race Team. I was especially enthusiastic about driving for chief mechanic, Jud Phillips. Jud was damn good, and there was no bullshit driving for Jud. You had to produce as a driver for Jud Phillips. He hated talking, he hated meetings, and he hated excuses. That's probably why we got along so well. It didn't take long for Jud and I to have our first "test" of trust.

My first race for Phillips was in Trenton, New Jersey. We had a rear-engine Gerhardt. I went out to qualify, and went down into the number three turn, hitting the brakes. The rear tires locked up, and the Gerhardt spun, hitting the wall hard. Uninjured and back at the pits, Jud asked me what happened. I told him, "The rear brakes locked up. Something's wrong with the brakes." I also knew that I'd better be right, because if I told Jud something wrong—if it truly was not the brakes—I might be out of a ride and fired on the spot.

Jud got the car back into the shop, checked it, and found that the brake balance bar had drifted off to one side. A little circlip that held the balance bar in place had come loose. When I went into turn three and hit the brakes, I had a bad balance in braking between front and rear. That's why the rear brakes locked up. Jud called me on the phone and said, "I just want you to know that you were right. I'm proud of you. You had every reason in the world to crash that car. It was our fault. The circlip came loose and the balance bar came loose and made your rear brakes lock up. That will never happen again."

That's the way Jud talked: no excuses; his people's error; here's the fix; end of conversation. No more whining, apologizing, or ducking nonsense. He was to the point and done.

By being accountable and responsible, Jud and I earned a mutual respect. I trusted him because he didn't duck his accountability. He trusted me because I didn't do something stupid with his car and try to blame someone else. I was honest with him about what happened, and after his investigation, he found out I was telling the truth. He could trust me with his racecars.

The other thing that clicked between Jud and me was the fact that I knew he gave 100 percent as a mechanic, and he knew I gave 100 percent as a driver.

Always Giving Full Effort

Some people may interpret full effort as commitment, but it goes beyond that. You are really building trust. In my last race for Dan Gurney in Phoenix in 1978, I knew I was quitting his team and going to work for Roger Penske as soon as the race was over. But I gave 100 percent during that race for Dan Gurney's All American Racers' Team, because that was the team I was on. In fact, I raced against Team Penske's Tom Sneva that day and beat him. I wasn't going to pull any favors for Penske, even though I was going there as soon as the race was over. And, I sure as hell wasn't going to give anything less than 100 percent for Dan Gurney and his All American Racers, because they all worked hard to get me there.

One thing that is truly American is giving 100 percent. That's what everybody likes, and that's why so many people pull for the underdog. People love to see effort, and they really love to see effort win. Nothing inspires trust more than a full commitment, for many employers, that *is* a big deal.

When I think about it, the people I really clicked with during my career always gave 100 percent. Don Shepherd was a perfect example of this. I raced sprint cars for Don from 1964 to 1967. I had been told to watch out for him because he had a temper and went through a lot of drivers. I didn't like turnover, so I kept my distance from him.

In 1964, I had just finished a sprint car race in St. Paul, Minnesota, and Shep (that's what we called him) point blank asked me if I wanted to drive his car. I was a little wary of this, because I knew Johnny Rutherford—a great driver—was his driver at that time. I told him, "Shep, I thought Johnny Rutherford drove for you."

He said, "I just fired him. He drives too dangerous. He's gonna crash really bad one of these times and I don't want that to happen while he's driving for me."

Fortunately, talking to Don Shepherd turned out to be entirely different than what I had expected.

I replied, "Well, OK, I'll buy that. You've got a driver."

Shep then said, "We'll race in two weeks in New Bremen, Ohio. I've got a commitment with somebody driving for me the night before in Allentown, Pennsylvania, but I'll make the race in time for your start in New Bremen, Ohio."

Two weeks later I flew my plane from Albuquerque to New Bremen, Ohio, for the race. I got to the track, but there was no sign of Don Shepherd. I waited for a while until it started getting pretty close to race time, and there was still no Shep. Another owner, Steve Stapp, had no driver for his car that day, and I agreed to drive for him. Hell, if I flew all the way from Albuquerque, I needed to race. I needed the money.

After I got fitted into the Stapp car, Shep pulled into the pit area, towing a wrecked car. He scrambled out and came up to me apologizing for being late, "Sorry, Bobby, but we had a wreck last night. I've been driving all night to get here, working on the car each time I stopped to get gasoline for the tow truck. I've almost got it ready to go.

I hear you got a ride with Steve Stapp. If you want to take his ride, go ahead. My car's still bent but I think we can get it ready to race. But if you have a ride with Steve Stapp, go ahead. I wouldn't blame you. I can get ready by the second warm-up session if you still want to run it."

If he got the car ready, there was no way I was going to drive for anybody but Shep that day. Anyone who puts in that kind of effort to get there, and still holds me blameless for looking at another ride—well, that's the kind of a person I wanted to drive for. When I drove sprint cars for the next three years, well over 150 races, I drove for Don Shepherd and nobody else. His effort earned my trust in him as an owner I wanted to drive for.

Actions That Back Up Your Words

I've always believed that the only way I could be successful and earn the trust of others was to take action. When you commit to something— do it. If you can't make it happen, don't commit to it.

If you want to be really successful, and have a reputation for being trustworthy, start out by making sure that whatever you commit to do, you do. Even if you have to stretch a little to make your commitment, get it done. Look at the long-standing relationship I had with Don Shepherd because he made it to the race, through hell and high water. Or the trust the car parts suppliers had in me for my 1959 Pikes Peak Hill Climb. I always paid their bills on time. I did what I said I was going to do. The return in long-term relationships built through actions that make your words true is immense.

Some leaders just like to say anything to appease everyone, but then they can't make things happen. Other leaders leave the dirty work to other people—they just give orders. Either way, that's lazy leadership, and in the end, unbelievable leadership.

The only way you can lead successfully is to motivate your people through your actions, not your words. Get involved with what your people do on a day-to-day basis. This is how you build real trust with your people. It is taking leadership action that not only shows you care, but brings reality to your leadership. When you are involved with your people, you know how to give them tasks that they will do, and do them right. They believe you because you have taken action to be with them, and, you know not to give them assignments they can't possibly finish.

You also have to be willing to take tough actions and make hard decisions. I had a guy working for me in my shop for 18 years, and I had to fire him for drinking during work hours. I caught him by accident. I was out running some noontime errands, and happened to see his truck parked in the parking lot of a bar. I went in, and there he was with a beer in his hand. I asked him what on earth he was doing, and he just said that it was no big deal, to have a couple of beers at lunch. Well, I sure as hell didn't let any pit crew members on my race team work on my car after having a few beers. I wasn't about to let one of my mechanics work on a customer's car after a few beers. It was an easy, clear-cut decision for me, and everybody knew it. So, I fired him. I had to. I had to take this action to earn the trust of the rest of the employees and my customers.

I could go on and on about trust, but let me mention just a few other important points here as they relate to losing trust.

LOSING TRUST: CRASHING AND BURNING

Look at all the people in the corporate world today who make it to the top, and then have to lie and cheat to stay there. Some of them even lie to get to the top. Why do they do this? From my racing experience, there are three causes for losing trust:

1. Impatience
2. Inability to deal with a fall from the top
3. Material desires exceed the passion for the game

Impatience

I didn't make it to the Indianapolis 500 until I was 29 years old. I had already been racing 15 years by that time, and had been in many hundreds of races. Despite that long apprenticeship in racing, I never really felt I took any short-cuts to get there. In fact, even the first year, 1963, I wasn't sure I was ready for Indianapolis.

What drives impatience? Why have we become a world driven by instant gratification? What's wrong with doing things *right*, instead of getting instant results? People want to see how quickly they can do things, including rising to the top of a profession. By being impatient, people don't get things done right—they'll skip steps. The bigger sacrifice is they may lie to cut corners. Getting the result becomes so important, that they lie and cheat their way up the ladder.

We've seen many people's careers ruined because they lied on their resumes. Why do they do this? They felt the result was more important than the means they took to get there. They justify the means, even if it means cheating and lying. Everybody has to pay his or her dues to get to the top. Nobody gets there for free. Part of paying your dues is to be honest about the path and steps you take to get there, which means you have to be patient. Some people who read this will think, "Bobby, you're one of the most impatient people I know. How can you talk about patience?" I'm not patient when it comes to taking action. I just know I can't take short-cuts or fake the results. You can be impatient about wanting to do things, but not at the expense of doing things right and truthfully.

Inability to Deal with a Fall from the Top

After I won the USAC National Racing Championship in 1968 and won the Indy 500, my brother Al asked me, "What are you going to do next year?"

I replied, "Well, I'm going to run for Bob Wilke and Leader Card Racing."

Al asked again, "What are you going to do next year?"

I said, "What the hell are you asking me, Al?!"

He said, "Well, you are the only one on top. The top is the very peak, and there's only room for one person up there. You are the champion. What are you going to do?"

I replied, "Well, I'm going to try my best to stay there!"

He said, "Yeah, but you probably can't stay on top."

I told him, "It's okay. I see what you're getting at, but maybe I won't fall too far. That way I don't have to kick so many asses to get back up there again. Don't you worry about that."

A lot of people get on top, and then they have to hold on for dear life. Some cheat to stay there because they're worried about falling. I knew I was going to fall. Everybody falls. That's the way life is. I accepted it. What I didn't do was deny the fact I would fall, and I didn't let myself get dejected when I fell. I knew I would get back up to the top again, and I did so in 1974, winning the Championship again.

Even in individual races, I often realized I wasn't going to win. Sometimes I had a car that just wasn't fast enough. We couldn't set it up any better and I couldn't get any more out of it. It just was not going to happen. That didn't mean we didn't run the race as hard as we could. Effort was never a question with me or the crew. We weren't going to get any more than our best effort could give us, and on a given day with a given car that wasn't going to be first place. I accepted that as a fact, but some people just can't do that. In fact, many corporations can't accept it either. When it looks like they can't "win," grow, or whatever measure they're using to show "success," they start playing with the numbers. Then the financial reports become fuzzy and on and on.

Material Desires Exceed Passion for the Game

What I learned from racing is that it is OK to fall now and then. You just have to get back up, but do so for the right reasons. That's a big problem with many people today. In many cases, material desire has exceeded the passion for the game. When your material wants drive you harder than your desire to excel, you're going to start losing.

The year I retired from racing, 1981, I was making $180,000 under contract plus over a million dollars in winnings. As soon as I quit, I had offers for $1,000,000 just for driving, *plus* my winnings! That was over five times what I was earning! But I didn't go back for the money. I knew better. I didn't quit because of the money, so why should I go back for the money?

Drivers today have long-term, high-dollar contracts. I believe that's wrong. It's wrong because they should have to prove themselves before they get rewarded. Drivers use the excuse that auto racing is a risky sport and they need to secure these long-term large contracts "just in case" something bad happens. To me, that's the risk they take for the big money they earn.

Pit stop at the 1981 Indy 500. Real teamwork in action. (*Photo courtesy of Indianapolis Motor Speedway*)

Sliding around a corner at Pikes Peak. (*Photo by George Lantz, courtesy of Bobby Unser*)

Holding the trophy I won driving my Cadillac-powered, supermodified in Albuquerque. (*Photo courtesy of Bobby Unser*)

I became the first driver to break the 170 mph barrier at Indianapolis (1968). (*Photo by Frank H. Fisse, courtesy of Bobby Unser*)

Me with Bob Wilke and Harry Nichols, of the Rislone Company, our sponsor. (*Photo courtesy of Bobby Unser*)

Tom Drisdale presenting me with a trophy for the Mid Season Championship. This was my first full season of racing. I was 16. I ended up winning the entire Southwestern Super Modified Championship. (*Photo courtesy of Bobby Unser*)

After winning the Pikes Peak Hill Climb. One of my 13 victories in that event. The Pikes Peak Hill Climb is the second oldest sanctioned race, the Indy 500 being the oldest. (*Photo courtesy of Bobby Unser*)

I set a land speed record in Bonneville. That white stuff is salt, not snow. (*Photo courtesy of Bobby Unser*)

BONNEVILLE SALT FLATS
Land Speed Record 223.709

Car Owner: ADT AUTOMOTIVE, INC.
Driver: BOBBY UNSER

Class: D/MGR
September 22, 1993

Probably the worst crash in Indy history (1964). Eddie Sachs and Dave McDonald were killed. (*Photo courtesy of Bobby Unser*)

Indianapolis 1964

Coming out of the 1964 Indy crash. My left tire is visible to the right of car 64. I am knocking Ronnie Duman (64) clear of the fire, saving his life. The car at the far left is Johnny Rutherford's, an eventual three-time Indy winner. (*Photo courtesy of Bobby Unser*)

My daughter Cindy as the trophy girl. The trophy girl didn't show up that night, so I volunteered Cindy. She cried because she didn't want to kiss a stranger after the race. So, I promised her before the race that I'd win. (*Photo by Dwight Vaccaro, courtesy of Bobby Unser*)

Receiving a trophy in Ascot Park in Los Angeles. The guy in the hat is J.C. "Aggie" Agajanian, a major race promoter and owner in the 1960s. (*Photo courtesy of Bobby Unser*)

Al (56) and I (92) in Pueblo, Colorado. I broke all the track records that day. Al came in second. (*Photo by Leroy Byers, courtesy of Bobby Unser*)

Tom "Little Red" Herrmann in the 1968 Indy 500 letting me know that all of Andy Granatelli's turbine cars were out of the race. (*Photo courtesy of Bobby Unser*)

Dan Gurney of All American Racers, and I made a helluva team. Dan was a genius in racecar design, and the numerous records we set with his famous Eagles proved it. (*Photo courtesy of Bobby Unser*)

Team work in action in Phoenix. My brother Al is working the jack. I relieved my older brother Louis who became too tired to continue driving. (*Photo by Mike Griffith, courtesy of Bobby Unser*)

The Grandview Motel really helped us out in 1959. (*Photo courtesy of Bobby Unser*)

I win Pikes Peak again and set another new record. Again, my thanks to the Grandview Motel for their help in making it possible. (*Photo by George Schellenberger, courtesy of Bobby Unser*)

The parade lap in the 1981 Indy 500. I have the pole position (right front). (*Photo courtesy of Indianapolis Motor Speedway*)

Speedway Park in the mid 1950's.
I'm running into Al Demaree.
(*Photo by Dan Roberts, courtesy
of Bobby Unser*)

Cooling off in Riverside, California
(1981). (*Photo courtesy of Bobby
Unser*)

Daddy's original garage and
service station in Albuquerque.
(*Photo courtesy of Bobby Unser*)

My brother Al and I getting a lesson in auto mechanics from our daddy. That's the first 3.8 liter Jaguar engine, which my daddy developed in 1956 by boring out a 3.5 liter Jaguar engine block. (*Photo courtesy of Bobby Unser*)

Studded tires for ice racing. This was for my ice race in Edmonton, Canada, which is the biggest ice race in the world. (*Photo courtesy of Bobby Unser*)

Teaching the Canadians a lesson about racing, even on ice. This is Edmonton, 1994 and I won every race I was in. (*Photo courtesy of Bobby Unser*)

You can see how dangerous Pikes Peak can be. This was 1974, the year Dodge announced the "kit car." The kit cars allowed you to order and build a racecar from a factory-made kit. (*Photo courtesy of Bobby Unser*)

The car I built and raced on Pikes Peak (1968). The cars would change, but the race was always dangerous. This is the car in which I won seven Pikes Peak Hill Climbs. (*Photo courtesy of Bobby Unser*)

A strategy session with Jerry Breon and Laurie Gerrish from Penske Racing. Two of the best! (*Photo by Hugh Baird, courtesy of Bobby Unser*)

No one thought that Daddy's 3.8 liter Jaguar engine in the Pikes Peak car would work. We obviously proved them wrong (1956). (*Photo courtesy of Bobby Unser*)

My crash in Phoenix in 1966, and what's left of the Vita Fresh Orange Juice car. The mangled steering wheel now hangs on my office wall as a reminder of how lucky I was that day. (*Photo courtesy of Bobby Unser*)

The Unser boys in 1945 after a parade. (From left to right: Bobby, Al, Louis, and Jerry.) (*Photo courtesy of Bobby Unser*)

1981 Indy 500 Winner's Circle. My third Indy Win. (*Photo by Al Behrman, courtesy of Bobby Unser*)

Winning the 1975 rain-shortened Indy 500. (*Photo courtesy of Indianapolis Motor Speedway*)

Roger Penske and me doing a wing change. Leaders like Roger Penske don't mind doing physical work (1980). (*Photo courtesy of Bobby Unser*)

Roger Penske taking charge at Indy (1981). (*Photo courtesy of Indianapolis Motor Speedway*)

This 1931 Pontiac was a Christmas present from Daddy and Mom to us boys in 1947. It became my second race car. (*Photo courtesy of Bobby Unser*)

My brothers and I sold five wild donkeys and used the money to buy this Model A Ford. (*Photo courtesy of Bobby Unser*)

My first super LaSalle-Powered modified racecar (1949). I finished 4th in my first race. (*Photo courtesy of Bobby Unser*)

Crisis management with Jud Phillips at the 1969 Indy 500. We discovered a cracked upper control arm. We were an inch away from a very bad crash. (*Photo courtesy of Bobby Unser*)

Andy Granatelli and me in my first Indy 500 in 1963. (*Photo courtesy of Indianapolis Motor Speedway*)

The car I drove in the NASCAR race for Nichols Engineering in 1974 at the Charlotte Motor Speedway. (*Photo courtesy of Bobby Unser*)

Don "Shep" Sheppard and me at one of our many sprint car victories. This is at Ascot Park in Los Angeles, California. (*Photo courtesy of Bobby Unser*)

My first Pikes Peak run in 1955 driving a supermodified that was converted at the last minute for this race. (*Photo courtesy of Bobby Unser*)

Bob Wilke's Leader Card race team in action, and my first Indy 500 victory in 1968. (*Photo courtesy of Indianapolis Motor Speedway*)

I have an airplane, and for some people, that's an extravagance. But the plane wasn't for showing off; it was for getting me to more races. I did it to support my passion. I know a lot of successful businesspeople that made a lot more money than I ever did and they are flat broke today. They let their material desires take over. Then when they had to feed their material appetite again, it was a win-at-all-costs proposition, which often involved cheating and lying. And somewhere along the way they forgot about the fun of the game they were playing—the desire to do the right thing the right way.

INTEGRITY

You earn a good reputation when trust is tested, tried, and found to be true. This happens over years of transactions and deals. An honest reputation leads to a principle of good moral character—integrity. This principle isn't just for individuals: it is also the characteristic of a group, business, and even a sport, like racing. In that case, it means holding to its principles all the actions taken by the sport, including the enforcement process and interpretation of its rules. Integrity can't be broken, even when put to the test as it was in the 1981 Indianapolis 500.

I won my third Indianapolis 500 in 1981, beating Mario Andretti by eight seconds. Afterwards, all hell broke loose, and for the wrong reasons. The day after the race, the USAC officials penalized me one lap for allegedly passing cars as I was leaving the pit area on lap 150, thus giving me second place and declaring Andretti the winner. The USAC decision and the six-month legal battle that followed could be a whole book unto itself.

No race in history had ever had an outcome changed the day after the race, and no such form of day-after-the-race penalty had ever been assessed in the history of the Indy 500. That decision in 1981 violated the integrity of the sport, and Roger Penske and I were not going to stand for such a terrible injustice.

Roger hired Jimmy Binns, from Philadelphia, the best attorney he could find. Binns learned everything he could about racing so he could be effective in our case. We were prepared to go to federal court, if necessary. The main points Binns argued to USAC were:

- The penalty assessed to the #3 car (mine) was extremely vague and not in any of the rule books.
- If the rule did exist, and to be enforced by the USAC officials as had been done to me, then many other drivers violated the same rule during that race, including Mario Andretti, who passed two cars coming out of the pits right behind me, A.J. Foyt, and many others.
- If there was a rule that was violated, the penalty should have been imposed at that moment during the race, as is done in NASCAR and all the other racing organizations worldwide.
- The #3 car was outrunning Mario Andretti's by a good margin during the whole race. Had the penalty been imposed at that time (lap 150), the #3 car could have easily made up and passed Mario probably within a few laps. Mario also had a tire deflation problem, slowing him down more as the race went on. Roger Penske testified, "We were never aware of the alleged infraction of the rules by my car #3 during any part of the race. Nobody advised me of even the possibility of any infraction. Had we known there was any question of a penalty, I would have given the information to Bobby and he would have driven accordingly and probably put a lap on Andretti."

It took six long months in the USAC Court of Appeals, but on October 8, 1981, the three-man USAC Appeals Board voted 2 to 1 to rightfully rescind the one lap penalty given to me the day after the race. I was also pleased that the USAC officials had not stacked the tribunal with their cronies as I had expected them to. The only questionable person they had on the tribunal was Charles Brockman, who, not surprisingly, was the one dissenting vote. Edwin Render and Reynold MacDonald were the other two gentlemen and were upstanding businessmen. They acted with a clear conscience, and I was given back the race I had rightfully won.

In the 2002 Indy 500, a near-similar situation occurred when Paul Tracy and Team Green protested the race results. Helio Castroneves would not have won the race if it weren't for an incredibly unfortunate accident late in the race that instantly brought out the yellow caution, which meant no one could pass. The accident was in another part of the track, and had nothing to do with Castroneves in first, and Tracy in second. Helio was slowing down because he was running out of fuel and Team Green knew this. At the moment when Paul Tracy was making his move to pass Helio, the accident happened and the yellow caution came out. No cars could pass under the caution, and by running at the slower speed Helio Castroneves was able to conserve fuel and finish the race. Team Green protested that Paul Tracy had passed before the yellow caution, but unfortunately, that is not what happened after a careful review. Tracy would have won the race for sure had it been run at full speed to the finish, but that is just the way things go. You can't call a penalty in a basketball game the day after the game and award the other team the championship trophy. It doesn't work that way in any sport or business situation.

You may be wondering why USAC would have made such a bad decision with my victory in 1981. Well, in my view, they did it for political reasons. They really didn't care about changing the outcome of the race and they didn't dislike me. They wanted to destroy CART. USAC was in charge of running all the Indy Car (also known as Championship Racing or Open-Wheel Racing) races in those days. In the 1970s, the drivers and the owners were fed up with the way USAC ran and marketed the Indy Car races. They saw USAC as a group of Good Ole Boys who didn't give a hoot about the sport of racing or the drivers. CART was formed to unify the car owners and drivers who cared about the sport and wanted to make racing better for everyone: drivers, owners, and fans. Essentially, CART was a major threat to USAC's existence.

Two people funded CART: Roger Penske and Pat Patrick. I drove for Roger Penske, and Mario Andretti drove for Pat Patrick. The reason CART drivers such as Mario and myself were allowed to drive in the Indy 500 was because we were the attraction for the fans. In the 1981 race, I finished first, and Mario finished second. The next day, a couple of USAC officials saw an opportunity to cause a big stir in CART, and maybe even destroy it. That opportunity was to start a fight between Roger Penske and Pat Patrick—the entire financial resources for CART—by changing the outcome of the race.

Again, without getting into the details of the long legal battle that followed, let me just say that Pat Patrick out-smarted the USAC officials and didn't take the bait. He didn't get into a fight with Roger Penske.

Pat accepted things as they were. He did it by standing by the sport of championship auto racing and his loyalty to CART. Pat held this in higher regard than an Indy 500 win offered by a bad political maneuver. As a matter of fact, Pat was elk hunting with me at my ranch in Northern New Mexico when the decision was finally made vindicating my win and placing Pat's driver Mario Andretti second. When we were told of the decision, I could see tears well up in Pat's eyes. He even gave me a big hug. He knew the right thing had been done and that CART had not only survived, but was even stronger. That's what integrity does for you.

A great example of integrity in the business world comes from a gentleman by the name of Mike Richardson. I met Mike through a corporate contract I had working with ADT Automotive Systems. For many years, the auto auction business in the United State was crooked. The main problem in the business was nearly everyone in the industry was manipulating the odometer readings on the cars, severely turning them back. Since the value of the car was determined by the presumed wear and tear, the fewer the miles on the odometer, the higher the value of the car. However, if the odometer on the car was turned back to a lower number, an unsuspecting buyer would be buying a worn out car with 90,000 miles on it, instead of a "low mileage vehicle" with 10,000 miles.

Everyone involved in the auto auction business knew this was going on, including the buyers at the auction. It was the buyers from the auction who then stung their unsuspecting customer, selling the car at a greatly inflated price. Enter Mike Richardson who had solved the same problem with the auto auction business in England. From this experience, Mike knew how to fix the problem. First, he understood that what United States law enforcement was trying to do to fix the problem was the wrong approach. They were trying to catch the people who were turning back the odometers. This was too difficult a task. What Mike learned in England was to focus on the buyers and sellers at the auction. His solution was to get laws passed to put the burden of criminal responsibility on the auction buyers and sellers, thus raising the stakes of culpability in selling a car with a falsified odometer. He changed the penalty from a misdemeanor slap on the wrist, to a felony that meant jail time.

Getting the legislation passed took time, but with the help of Senator Exon from Nebraska, laws were passed to raise the risk of selling or buying "clocked" (turned back) odometers to felony offenses. Now the people buying and selling at the auctions could no longer hide and say they didn't know—they were being held accountable. Overnight, the clocking of odometers went from approximately 80% violations to an astonishing 2 percent!

The other interesting thing that happened here was that with the law being passed that put the suspicious characters in the auto auction business on notice, the honest people who had been waiting for this business to straighten out came out of the woodwork in droves. This increased the sales margins of the cars the right way—through good old-fashioned supply and demand. With more buyers coming to the auctions, the sellers could get a better price for their cars. Everybody won—the buyers bought cars for their real value, and the sellers got a better price because there were more buyers. It's amazing that the very thing that the crooked people in the auto auction business were trying to do—make more money—was ultimately what really happened when the auto auction business became legitimate.

Integrity in business does generate profits. Fortunately there are decent people like Mike Richardson to show us the way. By the way, he became very successful and very wealthy, finally selling his company to ADT. Integrity is not only the right thing to do, it pays off in the long run.

As for people who didn't measure up to my level of integrity, I stopped doing business with them. I quit driving for Granatelli because he would promise things and not deliver on them. From 1963, when I first drove for Andy in my very first Indy 500, until the last one I drove for him in 1965, he always promised me things and never delivered. For example, he'd promise me that he'd have a racecar for me at all the other races on the open-wheel circuit. He never did it. Andy was only interested in the Indy 500, so for the rest of the year I was driving for Gordon Van Liew. After three Indy 500s, I detected a pattern and quit driving for Granatelli in 1966.

Trust is built and earned over a period of time. It is created through a series of circumstances and the principles by which you live your life.

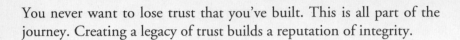

You never want to lose trust that you've built. This is all part of the journey. Creating a legacy of trust builds a reputation of integrity.

1968 The Winner's Circle Indianapolis Motor Speedway

I didn't take Granatelli's money offer. While standing up on the victory stand at Indy, I realized that I wouldn't have been there if I had. Winning my first Indy 500 was the greatest moment of my life. Not going against my word to Bob Wilke and the people of Goodyear despite Granatelli's intense pressure was one of the proudest moments of my life. I wound up having one of the longest contracts Goodyear ever had with a racecar driver. It just goes to show that you never know who's watching.

≡ PIT STOP POINTERS

- Trust is earned through actions that make your words believable.
- Stability in turbulent times comes from trust.
- Trust saves time in business dealings.
- Trust in others builds morale.
- You build trust by:
  - Being accountable
  - Giving 100 percent effort
  - Meeting commitments
  - Being involved with employees
- Temptations that challenge trust:
  - Impatience
  - Denial
  - Material desires
- Integrity is created when you build a legacy of being trustworthy.

CHAPTER EIGHT

ACCOUNTABILITY AND RESPONSIBILITY

Fall, 1959, Tulsa, Oklahoma

*O*n my way to a sprint car race in the Midwest, I stopped by John Zink's place in Tulsa, Oklahoma. He was one of the biggest car owners in those days, like Penske is today. He was a winner at Indianapolis a few times and I had bought the main parts for my first car—the Pikes Peak Pontiac-powered car—from him. He was a successful businessman in heating and cooling. When I stopped at his business, he said, "Bobby, I've got something new for you to try! It's a go-cart with two engines, with a throttle for each one. It's really fast. It's down at my shop. Have you got time to try it out?"

I didn't hesitate. "Let's go!"

I climbed into his go-cart, and took it out for a run. Not thinking there was any real danger driving a go-cart, I didn't wear a helmet. Wouldn't you know, I crashed smack into the wall of one of his buildings. My head cracked the wall so hard I was knocked unconscious. It turned out to be a terrible accident. When they got me to the hospital, the emergency staff thought I was going to die. After a few weeks of my being unconscious, even the doctors gave up.

I was out cold in the hospital for approximately three weeks. Then, one day I just woke up. I should have died, but didn't. I just woke up without even a headache, and didn't know what had happened.

Denny Moore, John Zink's racecar mechanic, and his wife, Virginia, were sitting there. I looked at her and said, "Where am I?"

She said, "You're in a hospital in Tulsa, Oklahoma."

Then I asked, "What am I doing here?"

She replied, "You don't know what happened to you?! Do you remember John Zink's go-cart?"

"Sure I do."

She said, "Well, you ran it into a building."

I didn't think much of it. It wasn't the first time I crashed. Then I jumped out of bed and said, "Well, time for me to go! I've got a Sprint car race to run in Indianapolis!"

Just then the doctor came in and talked to me. He told me how serious my injury was, and that I'd probably never race again. My eardrum was broken, skull cracked, and spinal fluid was running out through my eardrum. There would be a 90 percent chance of an infection, which would cause spinal meningitis. Half of my face was paralyzed, and one eye wouldn't close. That's when the Doctor told me I couldn't leave the hospital just yet.

I told him, "I've got to go. I've got things to do." And I didn't have enough money to stay in the hospital. To make matters worse, I was supposed to keep elevated at a 30-degree angle, and couldn't drive. So I called my brother, Al, and had him fly to Tulsa to drive me home to Albuquerque.

I wouldn't have dreamed of making John Zink pay for my expenses from that accident. That was my own obligation. I didn't have to drive that go-cart. He asked me if I wanted to, but I was the one with the choice of saying, "Yes" or "No." So, it's my responsibility for what happened after that. That wreck laid me up for over a year. I'm sure John Zink wished the problems I had would just go away, and I know he felt really bad about what happened, but it was my problem, not his. That's the Unser way of thinking. . . .

As you climb the pyramid of success, the space gets smaller. As the space shrinks, you'll find some people quit climbing, while others get knocked off for one reason or another. I won't discuss quitting, because I don't know what that means. When it comes to getting knocked off the pyramid, there are many reasons. One of them is people aren't as accountable or responsible as they ought to be. They push accountability off on other people or other things. What they don't realize is by doing so, they are jeopardizing their ascent, not helping it. To get to the very peak of any profession requires accepting ever more levels of accountability and responsibility.

In the last chapter, Trust and Integrity, I talk about how to deal with falling down. It's not bad to fall, because everybody falls. You just don't want to fall too far. When things go wrong, as they sometimes do, if you are accountable, you don't fall so far. Look at what happened with the Enron mess. Those people who were on top are going to fall all the way to the bottom. What are the odds of them getting back on top again? How far do they have to climb to get back up?

While trust and integrity is about being a person of your word through your actions, accountability and responsibility is about accepting the consequences of your actions. Some consequences are good, and you get rewarded. Some consequences are bad, and you are held responsible to correct the mistake or accept the result as it is.

First, a few parameters about how I view accountability and responsibility. Being accountable is accepting the consequences of the decisions you make and the actions you take. It's not passing the buck or ducking. You learn to accept a bad result, even if circumstances don't go your way. You can't go back and change the outcome. It's honoring your debts: paying people back what you owe them. It's the responsible delegation of authority: Empowering people with responsibility to make decisions and take actions, and to be accountable for the results of their decisions.

The Unser way is not to duck responsibility, but to stand there and accept the consequences. By doing so, you will also develop sharper focus, mature, and become wiser.

SHARPER FOCUS

You focus harder when you know you are responsible for results. In a race, I had to focus 100 yards down the track. At John Zink's place, losing focus caused me to crash. I goofed around. It was my fault, and nearly got me killed. Well, three weeks unconscious in a hospital, and a full year out of racing fixed that focus in a hurry.

What if I had run around blaming others and suing the hell out of John Zink, the doctors, and so on? I would have never driven a racecar again, and never won the Indy 500. I would have sat back and let some lawyer "fix" my problem, and would have wound up walking with a cane or being confined to a wheelchair. Too many people do that, and it's not right. If they stay focused because they hold themselves accountable, they can't help but to eventually succeed.

In 1967, when my daughter Cindy was nine years old, I took her to one of the midget car races. The trophy girl didn't show up, so I told Cindy she could be the trophy girl. The trophy girl not only hands the trophy to the winner; she also kisses the winner. Cindy cried. I asked her, "Why are you crying?"

She said, "Because I don't want to kiss a stranger!"

I answered, "Don't worry, honey. I'll win the race and you can kiss me."

I was committed and accountable. It sure made me focus and I won that race. There's a great photo of me holding the trophy with the trophy girl, my daughter Cindy.

In any of the races I *had* to win, or any of the ones that I was leading and were mine to lose, I focused extra hard. Losing a race, especially when I had financial obligations hanging over my head, just wasn't an option. In the 1959 Pikes Peak Hill Climb, I had to win to pay my bills. It was a terrible feeling, but it really made me focus. Once there was a good chance I could win the race, I sure didn't want to blow it, and made darn sure there were no mistakes.

MENTAL MATURITY

Have you ever wondered how people can "grow up" so quickly when they are thrust into war at the age of 18? Or suddenly a 16 year-old becomes the "man" of the family because his parents were killed? You can't help but to grow up when you don't have the choice but to grow up. Ducking responsibility is not an option. When you're in charge, you're in command. You mature in a hurry when you realize you're in charge, and do so because you are accountable for your actions. There's no other way to put it. If you aren't accountable, you can't grow. If you don't grow, you'll never be successful. You mature through the process of accepting responsibility.

I started racing at the age 15, going up against grown men two and three times my age. They weren't going to cut me any slack. Then, when I started winning, they *really* weren't going to cut me any slack. They couldn't believe some kid could whip their ass on the racetrack. They got tough with me, but I wouldn't back down. Backing down would have fired them up to go after me more. Besides, I wanted to win, and I figured out how to win despite their efforts to teach me a lesson. For me, it wasn't a lack of respect for them as much as it was growing up in a hurry to accept what was being dealt to me.

Have you ever been in an auto accident in which someone was injured? It's a pretty serious thing. An accident creates a situation in which people are tested as to whether they choose to grow up, or point fingers at others. An accident can be a dramatic life lesson, and it can play over and over in your mind. In auto racing, crashing is something drivers accept as a part of the sport. I've crashed many times. Some I've walked away from, others busted me up pretty bad, and a couple nearly killed me. After each crash, I learned something new and gained experience.

In your career, if you push the limits, something will invariably go wrong. You can't help it. It's going to happen. Accept it as a part of the game of growth and success. Most of all, when you learn to accept your responsibility for outcomes, you'll learn from your experience. These lessons will help you continue to grow.

BECOME WISER

As you learn to accept the outcomes of your actions (i.e., being a responsible person) you become smarter in the ways of living. You gain wisdom. Holding yourself accountable for your actions forces you to look at the deeper meaning of life, not the superficial meaning caused by lawsuits and blaming others for everything that goes wrong.

I was really nervous at 16 years old when my English teacher paraded me in front of the class to brag about the race I won over the weekend.

Thirteen years later in 1963 at the premier racing event in the world, the Indy 500, I wasn't quite as nervous, but still nervous. By the time I won my first Indy 500 in 1968, I knew what the limelight was all about. I had grown and become wiser. I had to in order to succeed and continue to succeed.

You'll be forced into situations in which you have to raise your level of performance, and thus your level of accountability. During this process, some things will go right and some things will go wrong. How you learn to accept things that go right is one thing, which I'll discuss in more detail in Chapter 10, Take Pride in Results. How you accept things that go wrong is equally important.

DEVELOPING RESPONSIBILITY

Thinking back on why I accepted responsibility for my actions, I had a good example to follow—my daddy. There was no ducking responsibility with him. He didn't make excuses, he didn't take excuses. That's the way he was, and that's the way I learned. Fortunately for me, my daddy was a good mentor on this subject.

What if you don't have a mentor? Well, there are other ways to learn about accepting consequences. I learned *a lot* about responsibility by racing the Pikes Peak Hill Climb. Going solo against the elements offered invaluable lessons.

Mother Nature is a great teacher in dealing with the reality of things and learning to accept good luck and bad luck. You can't point fingers at Mother Nature—she doesn't care. She'll keep right on being Mother Nature no matter what you try to do. At Pikes Peak, she'd whip my face with wind, rain, hail, sleet, and a blistering sun—and that's just for one race!

The other beauty of racing the Pikes Peak Hill Climb is you go solo. If there's an accident, well, guess whose fault it is? You can't blame another car—there is no other car. It is not the road's fault, the road can't move. You are alone in that race, and either you do well, or you don't. No excuses.

Other factors come into play as well on the Pikes Peak Hill Climb. Every once in a while there'd be some crazy fan standing a little too far out in the road, and I'd have to swerve a bit to avoid him. But, that was part of the race, too. One time coming around Brown Bush Corner a fan was standing in the middle of the road! I don't mean the side, the *middle* of the road! He wanted to get a good picture, I guess. Well, he nearly put me over the edge as I swerved to avoid him. I hope he got the picture after all that trouble.

In the 1967 race, the other drivers in the Championship Class had already gone on their runs, and I remember looking at their race times. It was easy to see I could win without any problem. With a good car and all my experience on this mountain, I could rightfully claim the Pikes Peak Hill Climb as *my* race on *my* mountain—I was going to win for sure. My brother Al came up to me before the race, and told me I had the race won, so I should take it easy. He added that setting a new record wasn't important—just win. I said, "Sure, no problem."

Al was my only competition that year, and he had dropped out during qualifying about two-thirds of the way up due to mechanical problems. Of course, as soon as my race started, I went flat out and totally forgot about taking it easy and the "guaranteed" win. Midway through the race, I hit a sharp rock while running a little too close to the edge and cut the right front tire. Well, some people would have blamed the Pikes Peak Hill Climb people for not cleaning the road so that wouldn't happen. Others would probably have sued the previous driver or the person who was the cause of that rock being there. A few ambitious folks no doubt would have figured out how to sue Mother Nature for cutting the tire. Racecar drivers wouldn't do this, and I know I wouldn't. The bottom line is this was my fault: the risk was mine, the actions were mine, and nobody knows how to control Mother Nature.

For me, Pikes Peak was my training ground for driving and accountability. It was simultaneously rewarding and challenging. The reward was winning the race. The challenge was to deal with the unpredictable and accept the consequences of whatever happened. You have to find your own "Pikes Peak Hill Climb challenge." You want to find something that forces you to look at yourself in the mirror and say,

"I am accountable for everything that happens in these circumstances. No hiding. No excuses."

Pikes Peak taught me to accept outcomes as they were, not how I wished they were. Sure, I'd get upset about a loss, but I never contested a race result. (The only time I got involved with a controversy after a race was after my 1981 Indy 500 win.)

BE ACCOUNTABLE TO THE TEAM

Now, you may think being accountable to a team is a topic that should be in the teamwork chapter, Chapter 6. However, if you are going to be an accountable person, that means you are accountable as an individual, as a leader of others, *and* as a team member.

In 1969 I got a call from Humpy Wheeler, the operator of the Charlotte Motor Speedway. This was well-before the present glory days of today's NASCAR. Back then, they had to struggle for credibility and to make ends meet. "Bobby, we want you to run in our NASCAR race in Charlotte."

I said, "Sure, what about a car?"

He said, "No problem, I'll call Junior Johnson. He'll have a good car for you."

Junior Johnson would have made me a really good car. He was one of the best stock car builders ever, but I had a problem. I was running USAC stock cars on the side for Ray Nichols. I felt obligated to Ray, and told Humpy I'd rather run Ray's car, even though I knew the car was inferior.

While practicing with Ray Nichols' car for the Charlotte race, my concerns about the car were confirmed. It became abundantly clear that I wasn't going to come close to qualifying for the race. The NASCAR people could see I was going to miss it. That was a problem, because they had advertised the fact that I was going to be in the race. They expected to have 100,000 fans there. Those fans would be a little upset if they didn't get to see what was advertised. A NASCAR official came over to my garage area and told me, "Mr. Unser, Mr. Wheeler would like to see you in his office."

I went to Humpy Wheeler's office. Bill Gazaway, head of the technical specifications for NASCAR was there, too. Bill asked me, "Bobby, are you going to make the race?"

"No way," I replied, "The car won't go fast enough."

I was just telling it like it was, not the way I hoped it would be. I wasn't trying to posture for anything—Ray's car wasn't going to make the race no matter what I did to it. That's not the first dog that bit me, so it was no big deal to me.

Humpy said, "Bobby, we've got to have you in the race."

I told him, "Humpy, it isn't going to happen. My car isn't going to go fast enough. I should have listened to you, but you know why I did what I did. I had to be loyal to Ray Nichols. I'm sorry about that, but I'm just not going to make the race. We're just not fast enough."

Gazaway said, "We've *got* to have you in the race."

I again replied, "It's not going to happen. My car *isn't* going to make it. My car is going as fast as it will go. We've tried absolutely, positively everything we can to make it, but it's not happening. I'm really, really sorry to let you folks down, but that's the way it is."

Humpy repeated, "Bobby, we've just got to have you in this race."

I said, "Well fine, but it's a little late to get one of Junior Johnson's cars, and I can't do this to Ray Nichols. That would be an embarrassment."

Finally, Gazaway said, "Go down there and tell your mechanics to take the nuts off the carburetor, unhook the throttle, and go have coffee. Tell them to take 30 minutes. When they come back, tell them to not touch the carburetor, just put it back on and that's it."

Well, if I couldn't get Ray's car into the race, Bill Gazaway would. I also knew there would be another shoe to drop on this issue, but was taking it one step at a time. I went back down to the garage and told Steve, my mechanic, "You guys get to have a 30 minute coffee break. Unhook that carburetor first."

Steve and the crew weren't stupid, either. They knew something was going to happen on their coffee break, and it wasn't going to be bad. They just had to do their job, and for 30 minutes, that job was to go have coffee and not ask questions.

When Steve and the crew came back they re-installed the carburetor. I took the car out for a few laps, and all of a sudden I was running qualifying times. I wasn't going to be the fastest, but I was certainly going to qualify. Now I had to wait for the other shoe to drop. What was my part of the deal for this favor?

I found Humpy Wheeler, and said, "Well, I'm qualified, boss. What do you want me to do?"

Humpy said, "You can't stay in the race very long."

The shoe had dropped. I asked, "How many laps do you want?"

"Not more than 20 laps," he answered.

I said, "No problem."

NASCAR had their advertising covered, I kept my deal with Ray Nichols and wasn't going to ruin it for the NASCAR regulars. Everybody won. I ran three laps, pulled in, and said my transmission broke. I knew my role, what to do, and did it. I didn't let the fans down, either, and made sure I signed a lot of autographs. I didn't try to rise above my role, nor try to dodge my accountability. Dodging responsibility—now there's something that really bothers me.

DODGING RESPONSIBILITY

There are too many people dodging responsibility by pushing blame off on others. The sad thing about this is it isn't just happening at the low end of the employee ranks. Executives and managers are passing the buck to protect themselves, often times merely by inaccessibility.

People who are inaccessible inhibit business. With some of my current corporate business dealings, if I get the gatekeeper treatment from some executive's staff person, that executive gets chewed on pretty hard when my call is finally put through. If they can't talk to people, how can they do business? Back in 1959, when I needed some parts for my Pontiac-engine racecar I was building for the Pikes Peak Hill Climb, I called Pontiac Headquarters in Detroit, Michigan, and was put through to the President of the company, Mr. Bunky Knutsen. When I called Goodyear in 1959 looking for a competitive racing tire to Firestone, I was put directly through to Gene McManus. No gatekeepers. No runaround. No voicemail. I got right through to people who took action and got results. If Goodyear had given me the run-around when I called about the Pikes Peak racing tires, they probably wouldn't be in the racing business. I would have called someone else.

I had a little health problem a year or two ago. It turned out not to be so bad, but I didn't know it at the time. I called a doctor in Albuquerque with a good reputation, but couldn't get through to him—the receptionist wouldn't let me. Her standard answer was to be crabby and say no. Finally, my wife, Lisa, went around her, got through to one of his nurses, and I got the appointment.

The first thing I did when I finally saw the doctor was to give him a good lecture about how his receptionist wouldn't let me get through. I told him he couldn't run a business that way and that his secretary was giving him a bad reputation. He looked at me and realized I was right and thanked me.

If you always keep buffers in business, how are you going to make correct decisions? I strongly believe that the number one reason people have automated systems and gatekeepers is because they don't want to be accountable. How can an executive avoid the very thing he expects his people to do: talk to each other? Leaders have to be accessible and accountable to be successful.

While a teenager, I wasn't comfortable with the notoriety gained from winning races, but as I grew older, I learned to accept it. In fact, I realized how important it was for me to be accessible to fans. I always signed as many autographs as possible. My phone number is still listed in the phone book (and has been all my life), and I answer it every time it rings. I don't view a ringing telephone as a potential problem, but rather as a potential opportunity.

I've asked many corporate executives why they don't have a real person answering the phone—someone who is not a gatekeeper. None of them has said it was because of cost. Not one of them. They're ducking responsibility.

Do you know why auto racing is the most popular spectator sport by far over any other spectator sport in the world? It's because the drivers and the people in the racing business don't separate themselves from their fans. Auto racing fans have a lot of access to the drivers and the teams. When you look at the racing business as a whole, you'll find a really good business model on how to stay close to your customers. The only barriers the racing business puts up are the ones that keep the cars from flying into the stands.

Another way leaders duck accountability is by passing the buck under the guise of delegation. They give a subordinate a no-win task that the leader himself would not do, and thus pass the accountability on to the subordinate. This isn't delegation—it's finding a scapegoat. This type of leadership wouldn't fly with any of my race teams, and it shouldn't in any business either.

Today we have executives who dump the tough tasks onto managers and just say, "Joe, you handle this." Then, when Joe can't get it handled, they say, "I'm sorry, Joe, but my board has informed me that the bad results of the job I gave you to do dictate that I have to let you go. No hard feelings, Joe. That's the way things go. I know these are circumstances out of your control, Joe." Circumstances? Joe was set up to fail by an unaccountable executive. It's sad, but this is happening in more big corporations than people realize.

BLAMING TECHNOLOGY

I am totally ashamed of the way technology in open-wheel racing has evolved to the point where the engineers are standing over the computer screens and making all the racing decisions. They are taking the driver out of the equation in terms of racing knowledge and racing variables. The driver doesn't have to do anything anymore but drive the car. He is becoming less and less accountable for knowing about how cars are built and run. And, because he is less accountable, he is less a hero to today's racing fans. Heroes take total accountability.

The human element *is* the interesting part of the sport. All the racing organizations ought to leave more thinking to the driver, because it helps the driver become a better and a smarter athlete. It also makes the fan smarter. A fan can't study a computer screen, but he can study a driver's stats. A smarter fan is a better fan, and a more interested fan.

In 1981, after my radio smoked, Team Penske had to go to sign boards. Every time I had to pit, I lost two or three positions and had to pass the same people again, risking fuel consumption. We were at a technological disadvantage, but we could still think.

During that race, I not only had to think about communicating with my pit crew, but had to watch what was going on in the race. Without the convenience of someone telling me over the radio who was pitting, who was gaining, or what place anyone else was in, I had to watch the scoring tower. I had no choice but to take over the race, and dictate how the race would be run. I had to mentally calculate when to make my next pit stop, adding and subtracting at 200 miles per hour. Drivers today don't take over a race. In fact they don't take charge on any lap until the very end.

Taking charge was what I was paid to do. I was *supposed* to be able to think. Today, because of technology, most of the burden of responsibility goes on the engineers. Who is going to make a hero out of an engineer in racing? You can't be a hero if you aren't accountable.

Similarly, technology is taking the shine off business executives. Many executives think that technology helps them, and in some ways it does. They have faster access to more information and can communicate with more people, even if they are in remote locations. Manufacturing technology helps businesses by increasing production speed, precision, quality, and improving flexibility. However, as leaders become more and more reliant on technology, they isolate themselves from what they are paid to do: lead. They make decisions based on the numbers. If a leader really knows his business—if he involves himself with his people and his customers—then he won't have to rely on the numbers to tell him what decisions he has to make. The numbers will merely quantify the decisions he knows to make before he even sees the numbers.

I'm constantly telling executives that they have to get their butts out from behind their desks and see what's going on in their businesses. They've got to get rid of the smoke screens and barriers and expose themselves to the rigors of their daily operations. They can't become corporate closet artists, hiding behind voicemail, gatekeepers, and technology-driven reports. All of these things remove them from the pulse and feel of the business. How can they make good business decisions if they have no feel for how the business drives? How can executives be motivated to win, if they can't feel the heat or hear the noise of the business engine? How can they be heroes if they aren't seen in battle?

HELP OTHERS SUCCEED BY HOLDING THEM ACCOUNTABLE

You can help people grow by giving them responsibility and holding them accountable for the results. I hear executives talk about delegating, empowering, and such, but some executives really don't get it. I've already discussed leaders who hide from accountability. One way they do this is by dumping the dirty work on subordinates. What about the other extreme? What about giving people work they're *supposed* to do, but they don't do it?

Some business people aren't comfortable with telling their employees to do their jobs, and then holding them accountable for doing it. They're afraid the employee won't be happy. When I was racing, my job wasn't to make people happy: my job was to make the car go faster, and if I pissed off a few people for making them do their job, that was just too bad. If you want to be an effective executive, you can't worry about making everyone happy. You can't make everyone happy, whatever that means. You really have two choices: One is to make some people mad for making them responsible for getting their jobs done. The other is to make the rest of the team mad because you are weak and didn't make the lazy people perform—then you've punished the hard workers by making them do the work the lazy ones didn't do.

Making people happy does not work. Holding them accountable does. I've been involved with audits by the IRS twice. I took on the IRS both times and won, but had to manage the process each time. During one of the audits, I fired my accountant. He wasn't a bad person, and wasn't a bad accountant. The problem was, he was afraid of the IRS. He wasn't going to be responsible for supporting me, his client. He had to go. I needed someone to stand up for me in my case, and not back down from his responsibility. It turns out that I was right, and the IRS was wrong. But my first accountant wanted to give them whatever they wanted, just to get them to go away.

Sometimes you just have to force people to be accountable. Many years ago I found out that a key mechanic on one of my race teams was smoking pot in the off-hours. Not that pot was such a bad thing, but during the racing or testing seasons, I had to have my crew members— especially the key ones—100 percent focused and accountable. My life depended on everyone being totally attuned to their respective jobs. Normally, what someone does off the job is none of my business, unless it could impact the job. As tough as it is in the short-term to help people by forcing accountability for what they are supposed to do, it's far better than the long-term problem caused by not helping people grow into responsible contributors.

I had a tough talk with this young mechanic, and told him to straighten up or I'd have him fired. Believe me, if the owner knew he was getting high, he would have been fired immediately. So he quit. And when I say quit, I mean the drugs, not the race team. He's now a chief mechanic on a leading race team because I gave him the opportunity to make a responsible decision, and he made it. He saw clearly the consequences of his actions, and he made the right choice.

Becoming successful means you have to do many things other people don't do. Being a responsible individual is one of those things. While some people think being accountable is a hard thing to do, it's still the right thing to do and a better way to do things. When you stand in there and take the heat of the battle, you'll become stronger, tougher, and better for it. You'll grow and you'll succeed.

Albuquerque, Spring 1960

. . . After the go-cart crash at Jack Zink's place, Al picked me up from the hospital and drove me home to Albuquerque. That accident took me out of racing for an entire year, but I still had to make a living. I had a wife and two kids to take care of, and they didn't stop eating because I stopped racing. I had a foreign car repair shop and worked from 8:00 A.M. until 10:00 P.M. six days a week while I tried to rehab. I had to get back into racing somehow.

Dr. Klevenoff in Albuquerque was the best neurosurgeon in the state. He took care of me, and wanted to charge me $35 a visit. I told him, "Doc, I can't pay you $35. I just don't have that kind of money."

He said, "How much can you afford?"

I told him, "I can probably pay $5 a visit, but I can't pay you that all the time, so even there I'd have to owe you some. Is that OK?"

Doc replied, "Yep, that's OK."

Dr. Klevenoff saw me through approximately six months of treatment, but I didn't improve. He gave up, and thought my face would be paralyzed for life. That wasn't an option for me. So I asked him who he would recommend to help me. He introduced me to a retired Air Force doctor who had a new way of stimulating muscles with electric shocks. This doctor charged me $3.50 a visit.

Pretty soon, I ran out of money to pay for that, too. I still had no movement on the one side of my face and my eye was stuck open, forcing me to wear a patch over it for protection (for over a year). Since I couldn't afford doctors or any type of therapy anymore, I had to do things myself— just like building my own racecars. When you can't afford to buy it, you do it yourself.

Every day, I would stand in front of a mirror and concentrate, trying to make my muscles in my face move. I tried to get the open eyelid to move, and spent weeks and weeks on that, trying every day. Then one day, I saw the eyelid move and kept at it. Eventually, I got total movement back in my whole face.

If it weren't for Dr. Klevenoff, I probably would have gotten meningitis. Even though he didn't get my muscles working, he helped make sure I didn't get worse. He probably kept me alive. If it weren't for the shock treatments stimulating my muscles, I probably wouldn't have been able to get them eventually to move through my own efforts. I didn't go back and sue either one of these doctors claiming it was their job to make me better. It was my job to make me better—I put myself in that condition. They were just trying to help.

By the way, seven years later in 1967, I won a USAC Midget Race in Albuquerque. Guess who came out of the stands to congratulate me? None other than Dr. Klevenoff, and he had tears of joy in his eyes.

If it wasn't for my accepting responsibility for my lot in life and the problems I caused by the crash that day, I would never have got better or got back into racing.

≡ PIT STOP POINTERS

- Be an accountable individual.
- Accountability helps you grow by
  - Forcing you to focus
  - Helping you mature
  - Turning maturity into wisdom
- You develop responsibility by subjecting yourself to challenges in which only you can be held accountable for the outcome.
- Be accountable to your team. Play your role as a team player.
- Be an accountable leader.
  - Don't duck behind screens.
  - Don't let technology control your business or career.
  - Don't dump your dirty work on others.
  - Hold others accountable for their tasks.

CHAPTER NINE

CHERISH FAILURE

Colorado, in the early 1960s

P*arnelli Jones and I were going to race in the Pikes Peak Hill Climb, but there were also a couple of midget races—one at the Lakeside Speedway in Denver, and another at the Colorado Springs Speedway— that I entered. With one of the best cars on the circuit, the Doug Carruthers midget, I had a good chance of winning both midget races before competing in the Hill Climb. Not only that, but with Parnelli Jones, one of the best midget drivers ever, helping me out with the setups and some coaching, the odds on winning were real good. He wasn't driving midgets anymore, but I still loved to race any chance I could get, including midgets.*

I won the first race in Lakeside, setting a track record. The next morning from six until nine, Parnelli and I were down at the Hill Climb practicing. That afternoon, we headed out to the Colorado Springs Speedway, a quarter mile track, for some practice. The midget race was the following night. After unloading the Carruthers midget, Parnelli asked me,

"Bobby, what's the track record?" (That's why I like Parnelli. He doesn't want to just win the race—he wants to break the track record.)

"I don't know for sure, let me ask one of the track workers."

I found the nearest worker and asked him about the record. He told me it was 15 seconds and 25 hundredths. I then told Parnelli, "The record is 15:25."

He said: "Okay Bobby, let's get our car set up to run in the low fifteens. We'll win big tomorrow."

"You bet!"

We couldn't get our time down where we wanted to no matter how hard we tried. We worked the whole afternoon trying to figure out what we did wrong, but no matter what, the best time we could do was in the high fifteens, not good enough to break 15:25. Finally, we loaded the car on the trailer and dejectedly left. . . .

If NASA can claim that the Apollo 13 mission was a successful failure because the astronauts came back alive, then I've had many successful failures in my career. Just like the astronauts push beyond the unknown in space, so do racecar drivers who want to win. And believe me, I wanted to win. But in order to win, I had to risk losing. I'm known for winning the Indy 500 three times, but there were 16 times I didn't. There are other drivers who tried many times and didn't even win the Indy 500 once, like Lloyd Ruby, who was one helluva driver.

The first thing I learned about accepting failure was to deal with reality. If you can accept the reality—things fail and bad things happen—then you can stop living in an excuse-driven world and continue toward success. Of course, you can't climb to new heights unless you're willing to try new things. The results of trying new things also depends on an outside influence you have no control over: luck. There's some good luck and some bad luck along the way, but that's all a part of the journey.

Once I understood failure as a part of the road to success, I became more assertive in my driving, and thus more decisive. I began to make quick decisions based on my driving experience rather than fearing failure. By doing so, I learned how to push and drive hard until I hit my limit. Everybody has a limit, and you need to find yours. But you can only find it by pushing to get there.

ACCEPT REALITY: BAD THINGS HAPPEN

In 1951, my daddy and I entered the Mexican Road Race as a driving team. I drove and he was the co-driver and navigator of our Jaguar. The Carrera-Pan Americana-Mexican Road Race, the official name for the race, started at the southern border of Mexico near Guatemala, in a town called Tuxla Gueterrez. It wound north for 1943 miles through jungles, mountains, deserts, and towns, finishing at the northern border of the United States at Ciudad Juarez. The race was held to promote the newly opened Pan-American Highway. It was a grueling five-day race.

They ran a staggered start, with vehicles flagged off one at a time— a few minutes between each. We went off as the ninety-first car. Even though the race was challenging with turns, heat, and mountains, there were times we could run on a nice, open straight and go about 130 miles per hour.

On the second day, we were in seventeenth and coming up to pass the car of millionaire Carlos Panini and his daughter, Terresita. She was the registered driver. However, Carlos was behind the wheel instead and was in ill-health. He shouldn't have been driving. He didn't even have a driver's license. The rules were that the slower car was to allow the faster car to pass if the faster car honked its horn. We were in the mountains, and I came up to Carlos and honked, but he wouldn't let me pass. This went on through about ten turns, with Carlos blocking me each time. We were probably doing about 90 miles per hour at this point. The next time I tried to pass him, he bumped my right-front fender, which almost pushed me off a sheer cliff to the left that was some 500 to 800 feet down. My left front tire went over the edge, but fortunately I regained control of the car. Carlos over-corrected his car to the right, and went straight into a solid rock wall. The car exploded on impact like an egg hitting a sidewalk. I didn't know it at the time, but Carlos was killed instantly.

One of the rules of the race was if you stopped to help anyone, you were automatically disqualified. The race organizers had ex–United States Air Force AT-6 planes observing the race, as well as emergency crews available. Seeing the explosive impact, I wanted to stop to help, but my daddy told me to keep going. He knew the rules and told me that people were there to help. That was hard for me—I slowed down to about 15 or 20 miles per hour. He insisted that I keep going, and grimly, I did.

We kept going, passing many more cars. Then we came to the town of Atlisco, about 17 miles from Puebla. I wrecked the car crashing into the town square. A Mexican Army General was there to watch the race. He told me we were in first place at the time, which I hadn't realized. We had passed 17 cars that day, but were then out of the race. We fixed the car just good enough to drive the additional 97 miles to Mexico City. When we got to Mexico City, I saw the evening newspapers that already had the headlines about the Panini accident. I learned a new Mexican word: *muerte* (*dead*).

Later that night, another driver, who was really my hero at the time, Lloyd Axle from Denver, came to our room. He was a great midget driver, and had had heard about the accident. He was one of the toughest drivers in the world, and had seen many drivers die in races. Lloyd heard through my dad that I was extremely upset about the accident. It was the first time I had been involved in a motor race where someone died. It was just Lloyd and I in the room; he talked to me for a long time. Lloyd was a tough, realistic veteran driver. He knew the risks of racing and told me it wasn't my fault, and that I shouldn't take it personally. He pointed out that Daddy and I could have been killed if it weren't for my driving.

Even with Lloyd Axle's reassurances, it was tough for me. The Mexican press accused me of being a murderer. Daddy and I repaired our car, and took the long drive home to Albuquerque from Mexico City. After we were home a few weeks, I was still feeling bad about the accident and the false accusations. I wasn't a murderer. Then the Mexican Government sent me a letter, in which they said aerial photos of the accident scene proved my innocence. The letter was both an apology and an invitation to the following year's race.

It was a terrible accident, but in the end, even the Mexican Government proved it wasn't my fault. Knowing that, along with Lloyd Axle's very stern and personal lecture, helped me to realize I needed to accept this one harsh reality of the sport I loved so much: people die in auto

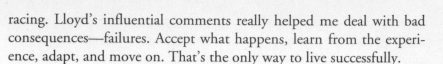

racing. Lloyd's influential comments really helped me deal with bad consequences—failures. Accept what happens, learn from the experience, adapt, and move on. That's the only way to live successfully.

Considering the fact a driver might die in any given race, anything else that happened during a race was no big deal, relatively speaking. You learned to deal with accidents, Mother Nature, fans standing in the road at Pikes Peak, and so on.

I'm a competitor, and want to win every time. When I was racing, I put a lot of effort into every race. I worked hard setting the car up beforehand, and drove as hard as I could during the race. But whatever happened, happened. Oftentimes I didn't win, and coming in second or worse didn't bother me. I learned something new, adapted, and got ready for the next race.

To be successful, you need to learn to deal with reality. It'll make things work a lot better for you in the long run. If you're accountable to shareholders, you won't have to manipulate numbers to change the results of quarterly earnings reports. If you're in sales, you know you don't always get the order. You've got to pick yourself up and go after the next one. That's the way things are. Give it all you've got today, but if you don't win, it's no big deal. If you're alive, that's a good thing, because you can come back tomorrow and try again.

Sometimes I'd be in a race where I was running behind the leader. Then my crew might radio me the news that I was gaining. They'd say, "You picked up two-tenths of a second on the last lap!" (or about 200 yards). I'd go a little harder then. On the next lap the crew might say, "You just picked up another half second!" I'd think, "Wow!" Then I'd push even harder, and the crew might tell me, "You picked up a whole second! You're really closing in on the lead now!" Then I'd think to myself, "Here we go!" I would come around the next turn and there would be the leader—I had him in my sights. All of a sudden he would just pull away and leave me. I pushed my racecar to the limits to catch him, and then he just pulled away. I wasn't going to catch him that day. He probably had too much car for me. There were many days I just wasn't going to win. Well, that's the way it goes. I'd just sit back and get what I could get. I accepted that second or whatever didn't look too bad in some races.

As much as I'm a highly driven person and want to win, I understand and accept reality. Some people don't understand reality, and that's what kills them in racing. It's also what kills a person's career in business. This is probably the most complex part of me for people to understand, yet it's so simple when you really think about it. I want to win very much, but I'm not willing to do stupid things just to win. I need to finish and stay alive, and race again tomorrow. You will be able to keep going on your journey when you accept the tough reality failure brings.

TRYING THINGS

Nothing happens until you do something. When you try something, you risk failure. That's the entrepreneurial spirit: trying things, failing, and then trying again. When we were kids, we watched our daddy try all kinds of things. So, we tried all kinds of things. For example, during World War II, we saw in a newsreel (there was no television then) that the government was offering $35 *an ounce* for rattlesnake venom. Well, there were plenty of rattlesnakes near our house on the west side of Albuquerque. Jerry and Louis were twelve, I was eleven, and Al was six years old. We thought we'd make it rich catching rattlesnakes and then milking them for their venom.

We took a one gallon Zerex Anti-Freeze jug, a few 30-caliber ammunition boxes, hopped into our Model A, and drove out into the high desert. Quickly, we caught about ten snakes—one we put in the Zerex jug, and the others went in the ammo boxes. The snakes needed to be kept alive to get their venom, so we put screens on the 30-caliber boxes and left the lid off the Zerex jug. Louis and I were supposed to be watching the snakes, but we were too busy looking outside for a few more. Suddenly, we saw the one rattler in the Zerex jug was about four inches out of the jug, and was getting ready to strike. All he needed to do was get out half way, and he could strike. We threw the jug out of the car and slowed the car to stop.

Not wanting to give up, we went back to where the jug landed. Amazingly, the jug didn't break, but the snake was gone. We searched a while, and found it, putting it back in the jug. This time we put a stick over the top of the jug to keep them from getting out again. Returning home, we put the snakes in their own 30-caliber ammo box with a custom-made screen door. We needed them to live until the morning when we were going to milk them.

The next morning, we went out to start milking the snakes, and couldn't believe what we saw. Every snake had been killed. A rattler attacked our dog when she was young and she didn't like snakes. She ripped open every ammo box and killed all the snakes by grabbing them right behind the head and shaking until they snapped. Well, that was the end of our rattlesnake venom business.

You try things to see what works. If something goes wrong, fix it and try again. Keep eliminating the excuses that prevent you from achieving your goal. I don't know how long it will take for you to be successful. I only know that you can't ever be successful until you learn to accept failure as a part of the process.

LUCK: GOOD AND BAD

When you commit to anything you need to look 100 yards down the track by preparing, by doing your homework, testing things, and coming up with a plan to win. Then put full effort into whatever the action is—racing, a sales call, building a factory, or making a cake. Once you've done that, you have to understand that there's another factor: luck. External things that you have absolutely no control over cause luck. There's good luck and there's bad luck. Don't get hung up on the result of any one event because you had some bad luck.

You have to learn to adapt and get back in the race. The next time you might wind up getting some good luck. In my first Indy 500 win in 1968, Tony Hulman said it was the greatest race he had ever seen in the Indy 500. I still had a little bit of luck when Joe Leonard's turbine flamed out near the end of the race. I probably would have caught him anyway, but his turbine failing didn't hurt. If you do enough things, and try enough times, you'll not only learn and get much better, but you'll see that eventually the good luck and the bad luck pretty much even out in the long run.

Sometimes I was involved in crashes that weren't my fault, like the bad ones in my first two Indy 500s—1963 and 1964. Other times a mechanic made a mistake—the brakes not set right at Trenton by Jud Phillips' crew, or when the pit crewman didn't fasten the wheel nut tight enough in Phoenix, causing my spectacular crash under the Armco steel guardrail. Those things are certainly a part of racing.

When I drove for Gordon Van Liew from 1963 through 1966, it seemed that we had nothing but bad luck. There'd be races where we would be leading, and something would just jump out and bite us. One time I was leading a race at Trenton, and things were looking real good. During the race, A.J. Watson came over to Gordon Van Liew and asked Gordon if we were running with short skirt pistons that day. Gordon said we were. A.J. informed Gordon that they had run some tests on those pistons and they failed after 115 laps. Sure enough, a piston broke, and we got bit again.

I would put a full effort in before and during the race, but I couldn't change the result. What I learned was that by putting in a whole lot of thought and effort before races, and working as hard as I could during races, I could live with the outcome, whatever that was. Sometimes I'd get lucky and win when I shouldn't have, and sometimes I'd get unlucky and lose a race I should have won. I raced in well over 1000 events, or including heat races, well over 4000 races. Over a long period of time and driving a lot of races, I wasn't discouraged by bad luck. Don't let a couple of bad breaks early on slow you down—keep going. Someday somebody else's turbine will flame out and you'll win one and deserve it, too.

BE DECISIVE

I've had to make quick decisions my entire life, and I am not afraid to make quick decisions today. When you accept failure as part of your growth to success, you learn to be decisive. Sometimes I'd be low on fuel near the end of a close race, and be faced with a choice. I either had to make another pit stop to get enough fuel to finish, or skip the pit stop and hope I had enough to finish the race. Sometimes I would choose to skip the pit stop and gamble because I'd rather take a chance on winning. When the opportunity to win was there, it was important to go for the victory. However, if I pitted to make sure I had enough fuel to finish, I'd definitely lose the lead and most likely the race.

In business, you have the same choices: risk resources to make the deadline, or stop, refuel, and miss the deadline. It's a tough decision because you may be risking quality in order to meet a deadline. I mentioned earlier in the book the problems with Harley-Davidson shipping junk to meet deadlines. However, just like in a race, you plan and prepare ahead of time to win, not come in second. I did say accepting second is a good thing to learn, because there are days you're just not fast enough to win. But you only accept second if it's necessary. Then you learn and come back raring to win again. If you continuously push off deadlines for the sake of quality, e.g., making sure you finish the race, you start to accept second place as a normal thing. Learning to accept second is a good thing based on circumstances, but it sure as hell can't be a long-term strategy. You want to win. It's OK to fail, it's OK to come in second, but it's not OK to accept that as your ultimate level of performance. Unfortunately, nobody remembers who came in second.

The contrasting styles of two Allied Generals from World War II illustrate this point—General Patton of the United States Army and General Montgomery of the British Army. While both were avid students of war, how they applied their lessons during battle was completely opposite. Patton always pushed his resources, risking possible loss if his resources ran short. Montgomery never even entered a battle unless he had a known overwhelming advantage. Patton always beat deadlines, Montgomery was always late. Patton won more territory in less time, with considerably less resources, than Montgomery. Patton always had a plan, and was always willing to risk losing in order to win, and he won more often than not.

You can't be afraid to make a quick decision. There are times when you simply won't have enough good information, but you still have to make a decision immediately—and you'll be held accountable for that decision. That's part of leadership. Many people hesitate because they're afraid of a bad result, and thus don't want to be accountable. That's not leading. In your career or business occupation, you are the leader—you are in charge of driving the car. People hold back on making a decision because they want to be sure, just like General Montgomery, but they never cover any ground, nor do they win many battles or meet many deadlines.

LEARN YOUR LIMITS

Now that I've got you going for it like Patton rolling through Sicily in World War II, realize that there are limitations to everyone's resources. Remember, General Patton was a good student of war—he studied war thoroughly, and always had a plan. He knew how to stretch his resources to the limit without breaking down. I pushed myself to an overload condition many times and had to back off from there.

Early in my career, I used to rebuild my engines every week. That was pushing it a little too far. That was overkill. I also developed ulcers; I would push myself so hard in preparation for a race, and then be worried to death the night before. My mom would find me doubled up in pain on my bed before a race. It turned out I had ulcers and had to learn to adjust things like my diet and how hard physically and mentally I pushed myself in certain situations. Even realizing this, I always had butterflies before races, like many athletes, but I learned how to keep them from being so bad that I couldn't stand up. I guess the good thing about pushing myself so hard was I truly found my limit, and had to back off a little bit from there. Just like running a race: If you know you have a lot more power than the other cars, you won't risk blowing an engine by running at its peak when you can win running a bit less.

The thing about learning your limits is you actually have to get there—push yourself to the limits—to know what they are. When I was driving the 1972 Indy 500 with Dan Gurney's super-fast Eagle, we pushed the limits of power and engineering way beyond what anybody else had ever done before to get more speed out of the car. The weak link this exposed was the magneto that shattered due to the harmonics from the engine. A $50 part failure cost us well over $300,000, but we learned, fixed the problem, and got better.

GET BACK IN THE FIGHT

You can fall, you can fail, and you can crash. You just have to get back up and get back behind the wheel. Nothing less. In the horrific 1964 Indy 500 fireball crash early in the race, (where Eddie Sachs and Dave MacDonald were killed) I got through the crash with bad burns on my neck. The Novi I was driving was totaled and out of that race, but my burns weren't going to keep me from trying to get back into the 500. It took about an hour and a half for the race officials to clear the track and restart the race. I went down to the pit area and slapped some oil on the back of my neck to cover the burns and cool it off.

I really wanted to get back on the track. As I was walking around, I ran into another car owner, Gordon Van Liew. His car was driven by Johnny Boyd, who wasn't involved in the wreck, and was unscathed. However, Johnny was rattled a little bit over the tragic accident and was not looking like he wanted to continue. I figured Johnny was done, and asked Gordon if I could have his ride. Boyd overheard this, and shouted, "No way! I saw Bobby Unser drive through that fire! He's crazy! He's not driving my car, no way!" Well, I guess I gave Johnny Boyd some crazy inspiration to get back in the saddle, because he decided to go ahead and race when they finally restarted. He wound up taking fifth, which isn't too bad at all.

If you want to grow or succeed in anything, you have to try new things and push to your limits. It can't happen any other way. Nobody is going to lay out a red carpet for you and let you waltz your way down. It's *your* path to success, not someone else's. Besides, how do they know where you're going? Nobody gets a free ride to success. You earn it, one failure at a time.

Colorado Springs Speedway, Midget Race Night

. . . Parnelli and I showed up at the track for the race the night following our failed attempts to break 15:25. We unloaded the Carruthers midget and tried a little more fine-tuning and adjustment before the race just to see if we could still get better times.

One of the track officials came over to us and asked how practice went the day before. I said, "Not good enough."

"What times were you running?"

"High fifteens."

"High fifteens?! That beats the track record of 16:25 by a wide margin! What more do you want?"

"16:25?! I thought the record was 15:25!"

Parnelli laughed until he was sore. "You mean to tell me we were going faster than the track record all afternoon in our practices?!"

And wouldn't you know it, we couldn't get the car to go nearly as fast in the race that night as we could in the afternoon practice session, but we still set a new track record and won anyhow.

Here we thought we were a couple of failures the afternoon before, when we were practicing, and we were actually succeeding.

≡ PIT STOP POINTERS

- Accept reality: Bad things happen, but they shouldn't deter you.
- Try things and learn from failure.
- Try more things. There's always luck: good and bad. The more you try things, the more you give good luck a chance to help.
- Assert yourself by making quick decisions.
- Push to your limits to find out where they are, then throttle back a little.
- Get back into the fight if you get knocked down. People notice effort after a fall.

CHAPTER TEN

TAKE PRIDE IN RESULTS

Indianapolis Motor Speedway, 1972

W*e had the fastest and most powerful car in the history of the Indy 500. Nobody was even close to the Eagle the All American Racers had designed, built, and tested. As soon as the race began, I took the lead and started to pull away from the field. My brother Al had won the previous two Indy 500s—1970 and 1971—and had another fast car in 1972. By the twenty-fifth lap, I lapped Al.*

Then, on the thirty-third lap, the Eagle's engine died—the magneto shattered and my race was over. Well, that was the end of my days as a driver for that afternoon.

I f there's one thing that ruins good, winning teams, it would be ego. Without question, ego destroys race teams and business relationships. Everybody has an egos; some are just bigger than others. Successful people learn how to manage their egos, no matter how big they are. They also know how to manage others who have overinflated self-esteem. The more successful you become, the more necessary it is for you to keep your feet on the ground. As you rise in rank, you will more often be involved with people who have overblown self-images.

Becoming successful, and the status and wealth that comes with it is one of the biggest causes of inflated egos. In 1955, Joe and Alan Foutz, a couple of drunks working a mine west of Albuquerque, discovered uranium. Then they became rich drunks. Since they had money burning holes in their pockets, why not get them to fund my racing for a while. They sponsored me, but it was a questionable arrangement from the beginning. They would come into a bar in town, get drunk, and tear the place apart. Then, they'd dump a pile of $100 bills on the counter, and tell the owner that was for the damage. It was pretty much a wild west situation with the Foutz brothers, but they were willing to give me money to drive, so I took it. I eventually found out they were betting on me around town, and that was not acceptable. I told them to take their big money and big egos for a hike.

I've always found that it's not only important to keep my own ego in check but also that of others. By being cognizant of your ego and others, you'll be more adept at recognizing potential problems arising from personal agendas, and be more inclined to let go of excess baggage from the past. Once you know how to keep egos in check, you'll see how to do something positive—help others succeed. This is a proactive way to stay grounded.

PERSONAL AGENDAS

Earlier I mentioned that one year the Pikes Peak Hill Climb organizers had declared recapped tires were not going to be allowed because they were a safety threat, effectively taking our advantage out of the race. My daddy then got a court injunction to stop the Hill Climb until the tire issue was resolved. However, he realized the race needed to go on as planned, so he dropped the case. He checked his ego—his individual desires to accomplish something—for the benefit of the race and the race teams participating as a whole.

What my daddy did was the right thing. He made his point when he got the injunction, but he didn't overdo it. He wasn't like someone next to a schoolyard who sues the school district to keep them from building a bigger playground for the kids because of the noise. Why did the guy move next to the schoolyard? Wasn't it there when he bought the house? Typically, it's just one person in the whole neighborhood who does this, and ruins it for everyone.

I've only been sued once in my life. One year a guard at the Indianapolis Motor Speedway claimed I shoved him and broke his shoulder. Nobody knows how he hurt his shoulder, but he claimed I was responsible and pressed charges. In addition to this false claim, it upset me that both my insurance company and the State Police investigating thought that I might have actually done something to the guy, albeit not as severe as he claimed. My presumed guilt by these people before I had my say really ticked me off.

The State Police wanted to get my view of the incident. How could I explain an incident I had no part in? That's like asking me to explain what it's like to walk on the moon—I just wasn't there. Then, my insurance company wanted me to settle out of court, just to get rid of the guy. To hell with that. I never believed in legal extortion, and wasn't about to start feeding the litigation monster in this country that does. It didn't matter to me what it was going to cost: I was going to fight for what was right. Principles are too damn precious, and this guy was violating some big ones—truth and justice.

I started digging into the "victim's" background, and so did the State Police, who figured out he was no saint. He had many problems including missed alimony payments and other debt problems. The case was dropped as a criminal investigation by the State, but the guy sued me for $1 million in a civil lawsuit. As good fortune would have it, somebody had taken a movie of the alleged "incident." A fan from Michigan had been shooting a video that showed I never touched the man. The plaintiff was a guy who tried to play on the American dream of helping the "little guy" battle big money: he was a little guy, and I was the big celebrity money he was after. A lot of people would have settled out of court and paid him off to make him go away. That's fundamentally unsound. It rewards the wrong person, punishes an innocent person, and encourages others to do the same. This "little guy" soon found out he picked the wrong celebrity to mess with.

Growing up poor in Albuquerque certainly qualifies me as an underdog. That's why I pull for the little guy to succeed. However, there are too many little people ruining it for business today by using the legal system to tie the business up in expensive, worthless lawsuits. There's a big difference between underdogs and little people. Underdogs try to

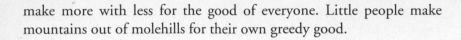

make more with less for the good of everyone. Little people make mountains out of molehills for their own greedy good.

GET OVER IT

Earlier in the book, I talked about the crisis we had the day before the 1959 Pikes Peak Hill Climb. Somebody had ratted on Al about his age, disqualifying him. It put Daddy and me in a bind, because now we had only one driver, but two cars. We were really upset about that incident. Who could have done that to us? Well, that somebody turned out to be none other than Uncle Louis Unser, my hero. Daddy was so mad he didn't talk to Uncle Louis for many years. I was mad, too, but what was done was done—right, wrong, or indifferent. There was no need to carry on the rest of my life about it.

The following year in the 1960 Pikes Peak Hill Climb, I was running the Pontiac-engine car, but was having all kinds of problems with the valve guides. Each day, after the morning practice run, my good friend and mechanic Howard Millican and I would tear the engine apart. Sure enough, the valve guides were shot. So were the cylinder heads. We were getting a steady supply of valve guides from my Pontiac engine parts (recall Bunky Knutsen's truckload of engines he shipped to me) in Albuquerque, but we needed to get the cylinder heads repaired locally in a Colorado Springs machine shop. We'd have to get them machined and then rebuild the heads before the next day's practice run. Guess who helped us machine the cylinder heads? Uncle Louis, at his shop in Colorado Springs, and he didn't charge me a dime. If he had charged me, I would have gladly paid him. What happened in 1959 was over and done with. This was 1960, and a whole new race.

I not only got past my issues with Uncle Louis, but realized why he might have told on Al. This is important when you're trying to figure out why people do something that isn't right. He didn't have any kids. Seeing his brother, Jerry, with four boys who could all race, was a bit much for Uncle Louis to take. Then, along came these young kids from Albuquerque to challenge him on his mountain. His ego couldn't handle that too well, so he told on Al.

Some people just can't let go of things from the past—they hang on to them and spend the rest of their lives justifying their anger and resentment. Holding on to that old baggage creates an extra burden to carry when you're trying to go forward. Cut it loose and get over things from the past. It will make it a lot easier to go forward. By the way, despite all the problems I had with the valve guides on the Pikes Peak Hill Climb, I won the race that year. I couldn't have done it without Uncle Louis' help. Dumping the baggage of the past race helped me win that year's race.

HELPING OTHERS SUCCEED

Another great way to hold your ego in check is by helping others. When you help others, you are really helping yourself, too. There are three common circumstances in which you can help others:

1. Passing the torch
2. Helping individuals succeed
3. Recognizing effort

Passing the Torch

In 1966, Bob Wilke hired me to drive on his number two team with Chief Mechanic A.J. Watson. His number one driver, Don Branson, could see the writing on the wall. Don knew I would eventually take his ride on the number one team with Jud Phillips. One day Don and I were flying in my plane, and he said, "I'm going to quit and tell Wilke that you ought to take my place on the number one team with Phillips." Then he looked at me and said with the deep, fatherly conviction, "Bobby, I want you to have my ride. I'm going to talk to Wilke about it."

I knew quitting was going to be tough for Don. Hell, quitting is tough for anyone. I told him, "Well, that's nice, but are you sure you want to do that?"

He replied, "That's what I'm going to do, and it's the right thing to do."

Don Branson was a man of his word. A couple of days later, he met with Jud and Bob, and told them he was quitting and they should give me his ride. It was an incredibly gracious thing Don did, not only for me, but he also took care of an issue that was concerning Wilke. Bob didn't want to fire Don, but he knew Don was past his prime and it was time for someone new, like me, to take over. There were so many good years between those two. Don's decision helped Wilke resolve what he must have been agonizing over, and at the same time gave someone new an opportunity to succeed: me. He didn't let his ego get in the way of doing the right thing for everyone.

Since retiring from racing, I've done a lot of consulting work for various companies. One of these companies is Mechanical Industries of Milwaukee, Wisconsin. The firm is a machine shop and contract manufacturing company for many of the United States' engine, water-craft, and motorcycle manufacturers. Its customers include Harley-Davidson, Briggs and Stratton, Mercury Marine, John Deere, and Outboard Marine (now Bombadier).

H.S. Hollnagel founded Mechanical Industries in 1948. He built the company and passed it on to his hard-working son, Harold Hollnagel. Harold is the person I worked with on my consulting projects. Harold is now preparing his son, David, to take over the company.

You may be thinking that the Hollnagel family business example is a poor one for passing the torch, compared to Don Branson passing his ride on to me, but it's not. First, each successive Hollnagel generation has continued the business' success and growth. Also, the company is heavily involved in the Milwaukee-area technical school development programs; it's interested in helping others succeed. The Hollnagels are a hard-working family, and everyone in the family has worked their way into the front office. This is leadership that knows how to carry the tra-dition forward.

Helping Individuals Succeed

Giving others the opportunity to succeed, like Don Branson did for me, is incredibly rewarding. I believe that part of being a winner is creating winners. In 1971, I had already qualified for the front row of the Indy 500. As the time trials were continuing, a good mechanic friend of mine, Wayne Leary, came over to me and said, "Bobby, we've got to help Roger." Roger meant Roger McCluskey, a good friend of Wayne's and mine. Helping Roger meant getting Roger over a psychological block. Roger was one helluva good race driver and could run all day long and compete with 32 other drivers, but running four, pressure-filled, flat-out laps all alone around the Speedway with approximately 250,000 people watching just psyched Roger out. Qualifying was the hardest thing to do at the Speedway. Everybody was watching *you*.

Wayne and I walked quickly toward Roger's car and talked to each other to get through the throng of autograph seekers. Roger was sitting in his car, waiting. He looked like a deer caught in the headlights. We walked up to his car and started tinkering with it without saying a word. Wayne adjusted the wings a little bit and I cranked more turbo-charger boost into his engine without him even seeing me make the adjustments. I had a short talk with him, telling him we had fixed his car, and to relax and just do what he knows how to do. Although we set up Roger's car to run faster, what we really accomplished was that we psyched Roger up by showing him we believed in him. Now all he had to do was believe in himself.

McCluskey went out and not only qualified his car, he did four 171-plus mile-per-hour laps. That was good enough to put him in the seventh row with his teammates Wally Dallenbach and Johnny Rutherford. My brother Al wound up winning that race. I crashed and wound up in twelfth. And good old Roger McCluskey? Well, he finished a very respectful ninth.

I had many businesses help me unselfishly during my career. A couple of companies generously supported me even when I was just starting out in my teens. Gene Stonecipher from the Perfect Circle Piston Ring Company, provided me with unlimited piston rings for free. Champion Spark Plugs gave an unlimited supply of spark plugs. Dutch Sproul of Sproul Homes sponsored my car when I didn't have a nickel to my name. They were incredibly generous in helping me succeed.

Recognizing Effort

While everybody likes public awards and accolades, the most effective recognition is the private one. You know, the unexpected one that isn't taken for granted: a personal phone call; or the private face-to-face handshake and thank you; the pat on the back punctuated with a quiet "Great job!" Racing sponsors were always thanked publicly for their support. Privately, their executives still liked the personal touch of the handshake and thanks.

There are different ways to recognize effort. Vic Holt, Chairman of the Board of Goodyear Tire and Rubber recognized in his own special way the effort I put in for the Goodyear Racing Division. There were a lot of cars using Goodyear tires, but before the start of each Indy 500, Vic would park his golf cart outside my garage in Gasoline Alley and wait for me, just to wish me luck in the race. The interesting thing about this is I didn't want anyone to wish me luck, but Vic Holt was my one exception. He didn't wish luck to many other drivers, but he did with me. He gave me his gold cross pin, which I still have today. It was mutual private recognition of good effort and thanks.

Sometimes there are too many people who need to be recognized, and the only way to do this is with a public event. In 1987, we went to the Wisconsin World Snowmobile Championship in Eagle River. This is the Indy 500 of snowmobile racing. I had a special deal worked out with our sponsor, George Walker, president of Armco Steel, the parent company of Chapparal Snowmobiles. This was my first snowmobile race, and the deal with George was if I led any part of that race, he had to throw a party. Little did he know the type of party I had in mind.

Well, I wound up leading most of the race, so then it was up to George to have a party to satisfy his end of the deal. I told George it had to be at his home in the Colorado mountains. He was shocked. Then I insisted that he invite everyone connected to the race team and the event. All the national snowmobile press was invited, and George paid their airfare. Anybody who had anything to do with building and running the snowmobiles was invited along with his or her family. This was a total team family event.

Fresh Maine lobster and shrimp were flown in the day before the party. We had the fabricators from George's race shop build special cookers for the lobsters. Hamburgers, hot dogs, sodas, and snacks for the kids were brought in along with custom-made grills and professional chefs. He also had to get three slot machines and bring them in from Las Vegas. The people received their thanks in a big, public way. What was really nice was we were still able to mingle with everyone and give everybody a personal thank you while eveyone was having a good time. That party was my paycheck for the race.

MANAGING EGOS

It's one thing to try to get a grip on your own ego. What about managing someone else's? The egos in racing can be enormous, but the same can be said for most fields. Lawyers, doctors, stock brokers—I can't think of any profession where egos don't have a tendency to run rampant. But excessive egos left unchecked can wreak havoc in any business. In my racing and business career, I've seen disastrous results because someone wanted to take all the credit and jeopardized the team morale. I've seen brilliant racing innovations not be approved because a senior manager believed that the only good ideas were his. And, I've seen terrible backstabbing by people trying to get ahead at another's expense. It always related back to ego.

That's the way it was when I was in the broadcasting business in the U.S. There were some people who wanted me to succeed, and others who did everything they could think of to make sure I failed. Of the people who wanted me to succeed, some genuinely liked me, and some had to protect their rear ends because they stuck their necks out to hire me. But that's the way it is in the American entertainment business—everyone is out for his or her own good, pushing a personal agenda at any cost, while keeping his or her own rear end protected. Only the individual matters and to hell with the team.

In contrast to the American broadcasting companies, CBC (Canadian Broadcasting Company) was an absolute, total team effort, with nobody trying to back-stab anybody else. As much as I hate government-run agencies and bureaucracies, working with the Government-owned

CBC was a very pleasant experience. Everyone treated everybody with respect.

When it came to managing egos, few were better than Bunky Knutsen, former General Manager of the Pontiac Division of General Motors. If you'll recall, I once called him on a whim, and he sent me a whole tractor trailer full of racing engines. Bunky made everyone hang up his ego at the door. He didn't give a damn about anybody's ego. Bunky told you what to do, and you buried your ego and did it.

In 1969, nine years after I called Bunky, I met him in person for the first time. I was in Daytona, racing for Smokey Yunick. Smokey and I were in the Goodyear VIP Racing Tower in turn four of Daytona, and Bunky Knutsen happened to be there as well. He was no longer with Pontiac—he had become the General Manager of Ford North America. Also in the room was Jack Pasinaw, who ran the Ford Motor Company Racing Division. Pasinaw and I didn't get along. I don't know why, we just didn't get along.

After we were introduced, Bunky and I started talking and reminiscing. Suddenly he looked at me and said, "How come you haven't run Pikes Peak for Ford? You know Parnelli Jones has the Pikes Peak record in a Mercury, and I'd like to have that record."

I replied, "If you want that record, we'll go get it. It's that simple. The only thing is, we'll have to do it the right way."

He said, "Of course we will! What do you want?"

Then I laid out what I needed to get the record for him. "Number one, I've got to have Smokey Yunick build the engines." Smokey was an independent engine builder, but he really only built Ford engines. He was standing not far from us. Bunky called over to him, "Smokey, come here. Bobby's going to run Pikes Peak for us, and he wants you to build his engines."

Smokey said, "If that's what you want Mr. Knutsen, that's what I'll do."

I said, "I need a special chassis. I don't think your Hulman and Moody people can do this one. I'd like Bill Stroppe out in Long Beach, California to do the chassis. He knows what I need and will do the job right."

Bunky answered, "No problem there. If you want Bill Stroppe to build the chassis, we'll get him to build it."

Then I said, "There's just one problem. Jack Pasinaw is not going to like this."

Bunky frowned a moment, then said, "Well, we'll take care of that right now."

Bunky wasn't going to let Jack's ego get in the way of making this thing happen.

Bunky called Pasinaw over, "Jack, come here a moment please."

Pasinaw came over and Bunky said, "Jack, you know Bobby Unser, don't you?"

Jack replied, "Yes, sir, I do."

"Well, he's going to run Pikes Peak for us. I want you to make sure Bobby gets whatever he needs for a budget, OK?"

Jack couldn't say anything but, "Yes, sir."

Bunky continued, "Smokey Yunick's going to build the engines and Bill Stroppe's going to build the car."

Now Pasinaw's hair stood up on his neck—he didn't like Smokey or Bill Stroppe.

I never asked for a penny, and Bunky never asked what I was going to charge. That's the way we did business in those days. He trusted me to do a good job at fair price, and I trusted him to give me what I needed.

As we were building the car, I called Pasinaw and told him I wanted a completely different transmission done with special gears. I didn't like the ratios in the standard design and needed to get off the turns quicker. We were going to use the 429 Boss engine, but I didn't want the four-speed standard transmission because it handled poorly in the turns. The automatic I wanted would be much smoother. Jack would have normally fought any such special request, but Bunky was clear on his instructions and my custom transmission was built with the ratios I had requested without any questions asked.

Bunky couldn't go to Colorado for the race, but he flew in everybody else from Ford. Jack Pasinaw and all the executives were there. Parnelli Jones had set the Hill Climb record in the Stock Car Class in 1964 with a time of 13:52. The record had held for five years, until I went up there and set the new record in 1969 with the Ford Torino built by Stroppe. I broke Parnelli's record by twelve seconds, running a time of 13:40.

I drove back down to the bottom of the hill, after setting the record, and called Bunky at his house from a pay phone. I said, "OK boss, you've got your record."

He said, "That's nice, Bobby, I'm real happy for you and our team. Just send me a bill for your services."

I said, "That's not a problem. The main problem is what you plan on doing with this racecar. Pasinaw will take it back to Hulman and Moody and it'll become a short-track car. That would be sad—this car should go in a showroom, or a museum, or something like that."

Bunky said, "Well, Bobby, the car is yours."

What a man! It practically brought me to tears. I didn't have a trailer, but Bill Stroppe did. I gave the car to him for his good work and great effort, and I knew he could be trusted to take good care of it. That car deserved a good home, and got it.

It's great doing business that way. There was no ego nonsense going on, nobody ruining it for anyone else or pushing his own personal agenda over what was required of the team effort. The focus was on one thing: win for the team—Ford Motor Company—and we won.

Make no mistake about it: we all have egos. I have an ego and it has helped propel me to the top of the racing world. Your ego will propel you to where you are going, but if you don't control it properly, you could have big problems. You need to figure out when and how to keep your ego checked. Every once in a while, you'll get some humble pie to eat. That happens to everyone.

Sure, you have to focus on the road immediately in front of you. But if you ever think you're bigger than the race, or that it's all about you, you'll fly off the edge of the mountain and crash. If you think you're the only one on the road, watch out—somebody is liable to park you in the stands and teach you a good lesson about road manners.

Relax, enjoy the ride, and help others along the way. When you get there, have a real nice party and invite everyone.

Indianapolis, 1972

. . . *"I came off of turn four and saw a new pit-crewman holding out the signboard," said Jerry Grant, another driver for Dan Gurney's All American Racers. "On the next lap, I pulled down into the pits. I could see the crew was ready, and I pulled in and stopped the Eagle for fuel and tires. I glanced around quickly to see who the new guy was on the signboard. Then I saw him: It was none other than Bobby Unser. He had led the race while he was in, but now that he was out, he wasn't sulking—he was helping me and my crew out."*

≡ PIT STOP POINTERS

- Avoid the isolation of self-centered attitudes.
- Release emotional weight by getting over things.
- Help yourself by helping others succeed.
- Give them the opportunity to lead just as you were given the opportunity.
- Increase the boost in other's careers.
- Recognize effort and teamwork.
- Command actions and results to lead over egos.

CHAPTER ELEVEN

EDUCATION
The Ultimate
Performance Enhancer

Newport Beach, California, 2002

"*B*obby may have not have finished high school, but he has an insatiable appetite for learning things," said Bruce Barnes, Bobby's agent and business partner for over 35 years. "I've never met anyone who asks more questions than Bobby Unser. From a business perspective, he's the sharpest sports celebrity I've worked with—and I've worked with quite a few good ones. If I book him for a company speech somewhere, he learns everything there is to know about them. He wants to know about their products, how they work, who uses them, and how they're made. Then he asks about the people and so on—I mean, he really gets involved. Nothing is part way with Bobby—he goes a full 110 percent on these projects because he really wants to educate himself. He loves to learn.

One time, he was out riding dune buggies and came across a few other people riding in the same area. They stopped and chatted a while, and Bobby started asking questions. After some time, one of the other drivers told Bobby about the great shock absorbers he had. Bobby took the dune *buggy out for a spin, and loved the ride. He looked at the shock to see who made it, and all he could find were the letters KYB.*

Bobby got back from his dune buggy trip and called me. He asked me to find out what company made the KYB shock absorbers and where he could get some. I dug around and made a few phone calls, but nobody had ever heard of KYB shocks. Finally, somebody called me back, and told me that I was probably looking for a Kayaba shock absorber. . . ."

I've talked about cherishing failure, and the fact that I've had many crashes in my career. Although each accident was a learning experience, the real trick was to learn how *not* to crash. Getting smarter before the next race was much less painful. Every aspect about your business you can learn will improve your chances for success. Education involves improving efficiency by training yourself on the techniques of your trade, and learning how to coordinate the various aspects of your craft to become effective. It's like the Penske philosophy of eliminating excuses, but with an education twist—learn *why* things happen, create new ideas, and *test* your theories; then learn *how* to make them better, eliminating excuses to fail.

For me as a professional racecar driver, learning wasn't just limited to driving: it included designing, building, setting up, and maintaining the racecars. Studying these other facets of the business helped me become a very competitive driver and win a lot of races. Anything I could learn to make the car go faster helped. If desire gave me a psychological edge, education gave me an intelligence edge. For some reason, I always felt that knowing how and why things worked seemed more important to me than to most of the other drivers. Of course, there was also the fact that learning new things was always fun and challenging for me.

You can put all the effort into anything you want, but without getting smarter, you're either going to burn out and quit, or get killed in the process (at least when it comes to racing). You can't get better without education.

People learn in different ways, and for me, I always asked questions, which sometimes drove people nuts. I felt it was better to drive them nuts asking what they thought was a pesky question rather than me getting killed learning the hard way.

Gaining an advantage on an opponent before a race started further drove my desire to create new car concepts. If I gained one-tenth of a second through each turn of the Indy 500 because of a couple of new ideas, that would be a very big advantage of four-and-a-half laps over the 200 lap race. What a huge advantage to have before the race started, and I would have taken it any time I could create it.

Each new and better way you allow yourself to master your craft increases your chance to succeed. I have been in over 4000 races, but they were mostly on the weekends. During the week, much more time was spent running hundreds of tests, practices, and simulated situations. Through all these tests, I learned more about driving cars, engineering, teamwork, and racing than most of my competitors—it often gave me a big edge.

Getting educated is a necessity. As an action-oriented person, I never really spent much time thinking about the *process* of learning. After thinking about it, there is a logical progression to learning. In the end, you want to be sufficiently educated about what you do so that you can teach others.

EDUCATING YOURSELF

Like everything else I've been discussing in this book, you can think and study all you want, but you don't really learn until you do something and see what happens. You have to *apply* your knowledge. The ultimate test of any plan for a race was the race itself. Of course, a lot of things had to be done before any race to help me gain an advantage. I discovered through my preparation for those four thousand races that there are five aspects of education that helped me win. They are:

1. Training to improve technical skills
2. Situational practice to simulate real conditions
3. Investigation
4. Testing
5. Analysis

Training to Improve Technical Skills

When my daddy made customized parts during World War II for the GIs that needed help with their cars, he made some of them on his lathe. I would watch him make special tools and then shape the steel and aluminum parts. Soon, it was time for me to learn. One thing I hold dear about watching people use their equipment is the fact that it's *their* equipment. They may show you how to do things, and may even let you use their tools sometime. However, as soon as I could, I always bought my own. A craftsman's tools are an extension of his skills, whether they are his tools, machines, computers, car, or anything else that is a part of his craft. Buying my own tools and learning how to use them was my way of showing respect for what they did and had accomplished.

Instead of using my daddy's lathe, I saved some money and bought my own. I would make all kinds of different cuts on it just to see what the lathe could do. Then I would experiment with different materials, cutting tools, and so on. After a while, my lathe setup was just right and it became a tool that helped me become a successful racecar driver.

Some people buy a tool and then let it sit idle. If you buy something that is going to help you, use it. If you don't, you've wasted your money. The equipment doesn't do you any good if it's not working for you. Just as you must have the right tools to do the job, you have to *use* them to get the job done. Have you ever watched a master craftsperson, like a glassblower, work with her tools? She uses flame, glass, special tools, and applies the right amount of air to create glass shapes and objects to perfection. She constantly practices her art, using different materials, temperatures, and tools to shape the glass. Before she started to make the piece being wrought in front of you, there were many private practices resulting in broken pieces.

Technical skill training is so incredibly important, yet so few people are willing to put in the necessary effort. Today, everyone wants the sizzle without worrying about the steak. You have to spend the time training to become efficient at what you do. Mastering skills allows you to do things quicker and better. By practicing the technical aspects of your craft, you can perform them without thinking about the steps. Your skills then become a natural part of what you do.

Situational Practice to Stimulate Real Conditions

I've said that the team that adapts the quickest during a race will most likely win. If you watch the teams that adapt the quickest, you'll also notice that they are the ones who *prepare* the most.

How does the whole system work? How does the whole team work? What possible situations can you prepare for so you are not surprised or panicked when they occur? These are just a few of the many questions you must constantly ask yourself. In racing, we often ran practice pit stops and emergency repair situations to simulate real conditions. Although we couldn't prepare for every possibility, practice helped us prepare for the most likely situations, keeping us sharp and more adept at solving problems we didn't anticipate.

Racetrack emergency crews prepare through hours and hours of practice. Today they are much better trained than they were back in the 1960s. Each individual on the emergency crew is trained for his specific task, and trained to do back-up duties if the situation calls for it. Then, they train as a team in simulated emergency situations. The drivers, firemen, and paramedics all know their roles and how to use their equipment. Most important, they know how to use their skills and equipment to function as a team when they get the call.

Nothing more dramatically illustrated the benefits of preparation than the efforts of the emergency crews during the CART American Memorial 500 held in Klettwitz, Germany, September 16, 2001. With 12 laps remaining in the race, the leader, Alex Zanardi, entered the pits. As he exited, his car spun out and was facing the wrong way. Barreling head-on at 200 miles per hour toward Zanardi was Alex Tagliani. Tagliani smashed through the cockpit of Zanardi's car, shearing the car in half, and shattering it into thousands of pieces. It exploded like a bomb without the fire.

CART's emergency paramedics and Drs. Steve Olvey and Terry Trammel went into immediate action to extract and stabilize the unconscious Zanardi from the wreckage. Although he eventually had both of his legs amputated above the knee, and had to be placed in an induced coma for several days, he did recover and has been walking with the help of artificial legs. The German doctors at the hospital where Zanardi recovered credited the quick response of the CART emergency team with saving his life. The training they went through was what made that possible.

That same thinking applies in real life, i.e., business. Before I give a presentation to any company I go through a similar training thought process. I ask myself: Who is the audience? What is the message I want to deliver? What information about the audience can I learn ahead of time? What are their concerns? What do they think? This is what I mean by doing your homework and educating yourself as much as possible. On some occasions, the night before a presentation, I'll even sneak into the room to get a feel for it, and visualize myself actually making the presentation. Finally, I'll spend some time preparing for the unexpected. What if the schedule changes? Suppose the projector or sound system fails. What is the plan of action then? This situational practice and preprogram planning helps make the real event go much better.

If you can practice or test-drive a system before a major event or deadline, do it. Situational practice will help make things run much smoother especially when things go wrong.

Investigation

Whenever I wanted to learn something new, I would ask people questions or go buy a book or two. To get more performance with better chassis setups out of my first rear-engine Pikes Peak car in 1962, I bought Colin Chapman's book on chassis design titled *Lotus Engineering*. It was a highly technical book, but helped me tremendously in my setups for rear-engine cars. Digging for knowledge by asking questions and reading books helped me get my homework done before my weekly final exam: a race.

Successful people I worked with did their homework, too. When I worked as the racing analyst for the two Indy car races per year with the CBC, I shared the booth with Brian Williams. Brian was the Toronto Blue Jays baseball team sportscaster, and hadn't really done anything in the area of motor racing broadcasts. To Brian's credit, he did his home-work ahead of our first scheduled race broadcast. He studied tapes, read books, and became a polished professional racing broadcaster *before* we did our first race. During a broadcast, Brian's strength was his ability to ask the right questions to play off my expertise at the right moments, without him sounding like someone who had never seen a race before. We just blew everybody else's TV ratings away—NBC, ABC, ESPN—all of them, mainly because Brian educated himself about racing, which made me look good, too.

You can also learn from studying how people do things in a different profession or business. I raced Formula One for a short time in Europe, and went to their races. I video-taped what they did to see if there were any lessons to be learned. Most of what I learned from watching Formula One was how their aerodynamic designs and chassis setups helped them gain an advantage in the various right- and left-hand turns of their race courses. This helped me in my setups for the championship (Indy car) road races. Other than that, the Formula One designs were not that much different than what we were using in the Indy Cars. Knowing that was a lesson itself.

As I did with Formula One, you can learn things from other markets that are similar to yours. The two-ply tire design, which became an au-tomotive standard, came out of the Goodyear racing design for our Pikes Peak car. The digital watches everyone wears today were devel-oped by NASA. Many safety innovations in standard cars were developed in the racing business. Look around, outside your own market to see what else you can learn, and apply it to your business. Why reinvent the wheel when someone has already made one? If you keep your eyes open for new opportunities to improve, you'll learn many good things. Learn to race smart, it's much less painful.

Testing

It's exciting to develop theories. Some ideas help you overcome ob-stacles and eliminate excuses. Others might create an important breakthrough, like Dan Gurney's Wicker Bill invention. The best part is to check theories out and to see what will really happen. We did this working with the aerodynamics of the cars. Wings on the car would help create more down force, helping us get through the turns faster. We changed the size of the wing, its shape, its placement, and its mounting. Testing these variables would help verify if our thinking was in the right direction. If not, then we'd learn something new and rethink our theory. Back to the drawing board. It's better to get a negative than nothing at all. Then you know in what direction to go next.

I loved testing, whether it was testing spark plugs, piston rings, or tires. It's like planting seeds. You think something will grow, but you don't know for sure until you plant the seed and see what happens. What are the best conditions—shade, sun, water, sandy soil, or cool temperatures? If you want to test all these situations for growing the seed to see which is best, you set up a way to simulate these situations. Plant several seeds and grow them in the different conditions. Water them, check them, and analyze what is happening. Each day something new sprouts or there's some other challenge, like a rabbit eating the leaves or bad weather. In the end, through your testing, you learn what works better and what doesn't work at all.

My brother Al and I lived across from each other (and still do) on old Highway 66 west of Albuquerque. He had a test track and I had one. It's dry in Albuquerque, and our tracks were dirt. When it was windy, and we were testing, we'd create a little dust bowl on either side of that legendary thoroughfare. The police knew what we were doing, so they'd just go down to the local coffee shop and have a few cups of coffee to pass the time until we finished our testing. People would come into the coffee shop and complain about the dust being kicked up. The police would look at the clock, and then say they'd "check it out in a little while." That was usually about an hour or two, but by then we would be done and the dust clouds gone.

Realistically, I might have tested more tires than any person dead or alive. Tires were the major key to more speed. Of course, tires weren't the only part of the car. Other components were tested and developed, such as new chassis setups, spark plugs, piston rings, and aerodynamics. Checking how things work was the only way to see if any ideas were right, or if it was true in certain conditions. Most drivers charged for testing, but I did it for free, because it was fun and very necessary to learn something new. Moreover, the objective was always to win races, and anything that would gain an advantage in winning a race was well worth doing. I found testing was another way to gain an advantage, so I did a lot of it—and loved doing it.

Whatever you do in life or your career, you've always got to try new things. Experiment with things to see how you can improve whatever you do. That's how inventions are made. Dan Gurney was always trying new things—new ways to make a car go faster. That's why we set speed record after speed record in the 1970s. By creating and experimenting, you will most likely lead the way.

Analysis

After testing was done, I would study what happened to figure out how to make the car go even faster. Earlier in the book I talked about how the Pikes Peak Hill Climb organizers had ticked Daddy and me off by not letting us use the recapped tires. That's when I got involved with Goodyear and called Gene McManus and asked him to create walnut impregenated tires. From my conversations with Gene, he was able to come up with a few samples to try with different size shells. After all, neither of us knew which size was best. Once we tested and learned what size walnut shell worked best, we started to look at other design features of the tires. We worked on a two-ply design, and then started changing the angle in which the cords were laid. Material was removed to reduce weight. We'd test each different tire and analyze it to figure out what worked best, looking for the best traction.

Testing tires was a straightforward process of elimination. We'd try a couple of things, see which didn't work and which did, and use that. It was time-consuming, but very simple. Sometimes, however, checking out new ideas wasn't as straightforward as that, because making one change often affected other components in the system.

For example, another way to increase tire friction on the road— other than the makeup of the tire itself—was to find ways to push the car down harder on the surface. We could add weight and let gravity do the trick, but added weight slows the car down and eats more gas. In fact, weight was a very bad thing in a car, and we did everything we could to take weight out.

Creating additional downward forces on the car was done primarily in two other ways: ground effects and aerodynamics. The ground effects force was caused by the velocity of the air under the car being different than the air moving around the car, which created a vacuum that literally sucked the car down on to the road. By modifying the underbelly design of the car, the amount and placement of the ground effect suction could be changed. For the other downward force, aerodynamics, we designed wings to take advantage of the air rushing over the car. However, wings created drag, and drag is exactly what its name implies: it slows you down. So, it wasn't as simple as just designing a wide wing and sticking it up in the air to maximize the downward force. There had to be a happy medium between how much wing we could take advantage of without creating too much drag. Then we had to balance where we placed the wing with where we wanted the ground effects suction. These were interactive concepts that weren't simply tested by a process of elimination. It required intuitive analysis.

If you make a product, you know that changing any part of the manufacturing process will affect other things in the system. When you increase performance in one area, it sometimes exposes a flaw in another. This is a natural process of trying things and analyzing what happens. A problem gets fixed in one area, and something else slips in performance in another. Step back and see how the whole system performs with an adjustment in any one area. This process will force you to think analytically about how the whole system functions. This creates thinking that is focused on treating the disease, not just the symptom.

How you improve the things you do requires such interactive thinking. It's not just a matter of *reacting* quickly to fix things: it's a matter of *adapting* the quickest to win. When you react, you fix old problems and can only be as good as you were. When you adapt, you create new ideas that can make you better.

PASSING ON THE KNOWLEDGE: WHEN THE PUPIL BECOMES THE TEACHER

Education isn't just about learning: it also involves teaching. You need to get involved with the people around you and one way to do so is to teach them what you've learned. Training people forces *you* to do things right. If you want to test how much you know about something, train someone else.

There are three amazing benefits to helping others learn. First, teaching forces you to show others the right way to do something. Second, it gives someone an opportunity to learn. The third benefit is that it creates outside-the-box thinking. While the second two benefits imply helping others (which is good), you'll see in the following examples, that these will ultimately help you as well.

Show Them the Right Way

When you teach someone, you have to show him all the details, and every detail done the right way. Your student will watch every step you make, so no corners can be cut and no technique done wrong. The words and the actions have to be correct all the way through the whole process. Saying one thing and doing another is not going to work.

This is also a good time to bring up a very important point: Do the right thing the right way all the time, because you never know who's watching. Leaders can talk all they want about what they want their people to do and how they want their people to do it, but people will *observe* what the leader does. Effective leaders are great teachers, and great teachers practice what they preach.

In my business work as a TV color analyst, Dennis Swanson, then President of ABC Sports, was a great leader who was also a great teacher. He totally immersed himself in his people's activities, not because he wanted to micromanage every little detail, but because he cared enough to teach them the right way to do things. He encouraged his people to do the same and show others the right way. Dennis was a successful leader as the head of ABC Sports, he took it from being a loser to being a winner and his track record over the years proved it.

Sometimes you can put someone in the position of trainer by asking him questions about what he is doing. I don't mean you should be nosy. Ask questions to *learn* from him. You can learn from anybody. By asking questions, more often than not, you'll get a better job done.

I hired someone to lay tile in my garage. I asked him a lot of questions about the different aspects of laying tile. What kind of glue was he going to use? How does he work the corners? The questioning didn't interfere with his ability to get his work done. After a few more questions, he realized I was genuinely interested in his work and wanted to learn. Then, he took over and started to teach me as he laid the tile. He narrated each thing he did, telling me what he was doing and why he was doing it one step at a time, and then what the next step was. He told me about the things to watch out for, and a little secret or two he learned about the trade. When it was all finished, he had been a teacher, I had learned something, and the best thing of all was it was a damn good job.

Give Someone an Opportunity to Learn

Holding on to your knowledge is a waste. We all have something we've learned through our experiences that we can pass on to others to help them. Of course, it's understood that some people just won't listen or learn. They fall into the category of people who live in denial, learn the hard way, or crash and burn their careers. I'm more interested in training people who *want* to learn.

You'll never go wrong when you pass on your well-earned wisdom to others who are eager to learn. When Parnelli Jones came to Pikes Peak to race in 1962, I helped him set up his racecar for the Hill Climb. There I was, Bobby Unser, from Albuquerque, New Mexico, showing one of the greatest racecar drivers ever, Parnelli Jones, how to do things. That's why Parnelli was one of the best drivers. He was never afraid to learn from anyone. He knew I had a lot of experience and knowledge on the Hill Climb and wasn't afraid to ask questions and learn. Parnelli turned out to be a pretty good student, he took third that year in the Stock Division Race, and then won it the next year with a record time. Perhaps I'd have won if I didn't help Parnelli out and share my secrets with him. But such thinking and second-guessing is not the Unser way.

What goes around comes around. And it certainly came around in 1963 when Parnelli showed an interest in my racing abilities by recommending me as a driver for the Indianapolis 500. Doing the right things for the right reasons always pays off down the road. Giving someone an opportunity to learn from your experience is doing the right thing for the right reason, and it too, will eventually pay off.

Get Them to Think Outside the Box

Real teaching involves not just showing someone the right way to do something, but turning on that light bulb so the person starts to think outside the box. Roger Penske has been and remains a very effective leader this way. He encourages people to innovate and think creatively. My experience with Roger was no different. Remember the last-minute test we had to run on the PC-7 in Ontario, California before going to Indianapolis? Roger was "boxed in" time-wise, but he didn't discourage me from presenting my case. Then there was the wing modification I wanted built for the PC-8 on short notice before the following Indy 500. I drew my own mental time box on that one, because I didn't think he could get the wing done in time for qualifying. Roger knocked down my own walls when he pulled out a piece of paper and told me to design the wing. That's how he gets so many things done and has built a multi-billion dollar corporation. He doesn't do it all himself, but he certainly attracts good people. He teaches them the Penske way of eliminating excuses, and encourages them to learn, adapt, and get better. He is the greatest trainer I ever worked with.

As I look around at corporate America, I can't help but notice that too many people are given restrictive instruction today. They're all given tiny boxes in which to work, with no room for innovation. If they try to venture outside the box, they are punished with more restrictive workplace rules. Even worse, the box is made smaller. Creating walls and then making the box smaller doesn't educate anyone. In fact, it is the opposite of teaching. Helping people learn breaks down barriers and opens new horizons.

Today, much of my time is spent testifying as an expert witness on automotive engineering issues in accident cases. In many of these cases, tens of millions of dollars are at stake. Here I am, without a high school diploma, taking the stand as an expert witness. I just love when the opposing counsel seeks to challenge my credibility. How little they realize how much I enjoy the learning and education process. In many of my cases, I think it's not an exaggeration to say I knew more about the cases than many of the lawyers. Over the years, the word has gotten around in the litigation community that the last thing a lawyer ought to do is challenge Bobby Unser's qualifications as an expert witness.

A desire to do something successfully cannot be accomplished without a desire to learn how to do it. I always wanted to win, but I didn't wait for the race to start to work on winning. Educating myself before a race gave me an advantage before the race even started. Testing, testing, and more testing; simulating race conditions like I did often on my test track in Albuquerque; or driving slow in a passenger car up the Pikes Peak Hill Climb, memorizing every turn. Anything I could do to win a race before it started helped.

Use education to get an advantage. Watch people in your profession and ask questions to learn why they do things a certain way. Develop new ideas, test your theories, and analyze the results. Once you've done that, try to figure out how to improve yourself more. Then, pass on your knowledge by teaching others to help them become winners. Challenge yourself to get smarter, and you'll certainly increase your chances to succeed.

. . . Newport Beach, California

"I investigated further, and found out that Kayaba was in Japan. I got the phone number and called the company. It turned out that it was actually just setting up an organization to market shock absorbers in the United States. The timing was perfect on our part. Kayaba said it had some shock absorbers in the basement of the Japanese Consulate in Los Angeles and referred me to Buck Bradley as a United States contact. Bradley and I went to the consulate, and a few consulate people helped us find them. They were really good shocks, so now we chased Kayaba to help it set up its United States marketing program.

After a few meetings and discussions with Zen Ishikawa, Kayaba Vice President of Marketing, and Jack Dannenberg, the Kayaba North American national sales manager, whose office was in Chicago, we went forward with an endorsement contract that eventually lasted for nine years. The United States product launch was in 1976 at the Conrad-Hilton in Chicago and was a huge success! Bobby had just won his second Indy 500 the year before, and with him at the event, we drew over 200 aftermarket distributors.

It all started because Bobby asked questions about things to learn something new. I guess I have picked up on this habit, too, because I had to ask a lot of questions to find these people and make the marketing deal happen."

☰ PIT STOP POINTERS

- Use education to gain an advantage.
- Find a willing teacher: watch, ask questions, and learn.
- Apply your knowledge by testing, training, and simulating real conditions.
- Pass on your experience so that others may learn.

CHAPTER TWELVE

THE FAMILY WILDCARD

Albuquerque, New Mexico

"*I came up to an intersection, and the light was red. So I stopped,*" *said Parnelli Jones.*

"*Bobby said, 'Don't worry Parnelli, I know all the cops in town. It's OK, go ahead and go through the red light. You won't get a ticket.'*

"*I hesitated, but thought, 'What the heck.' I drove through the red light.*

"*We cruised along and came up to another red light. Instinctively, I braked. Bobby said, 'No, no, Parnelli! Keep going! Trust me, I know the cops in this town. You won't get a ticket!'*

"*So, I went through that light. At the next red light, before I could even think about braking, Bobby said, 'Trust me, Parnelli. You won't get a ticket.'*

"*Finally, I believed him. So, I proceeded to drive through the next three lights in a row, all of which were red. I was thinking, 'What a family he has here in Albuquerque, all these Unsers. I'm starting to feel like a part of the family, too. A surrogate Unser. . . .'*"

Your family, literally and figuratively, can help you enormously and you should look to them for support. If you don't have blood relatives directly connected with your career and objectives, you probably have a "family" of peers, associates, and mentors. The trusted circle—

the business family—is a great asset in the development of any success-ful career or business undertaking. They are there when things get tough, or you need that extra help to get going.

The family of Unsers was the first crew I had for racing, but every-one who was added to crew that wasn't family became family. They were an extension of the Unsers. It goes beyond that family, too. There were the owners, like Ozzie Olson, Earle Jorgensen, Bob Wilke, Dan Gur-ney, Roger Penkse, Gordon Van Liew, and the many midget and sprint car owners I drove for. Mechanics like Howard Millican, Jim McGee, Laurie Garrish, Jerry Breton, and Wayne Leary were family, and they built some great cars for me to drive. Racing has its family of drivers too, like Parnelli Jones, A.J. Foyt, Roger McCluskey, my brother, Al, and Mario Andretti. Then there are the fans—lots of fans who become a part of the family. The racing fraternity is one, big close-knit family.

THE RACING FAMILY UNSER

The racing family is a unique family. To understand and support a ca-reer where your dad, husband, father, or brother gets into a racecar and may not come back in one piece makes the family life exciting, often-times nervous, and when the situation calls for it, exceptionally close.

I've talked a lot about my daddy already in this book, so you know the significant role he played. Mom was equally important, but in a dif-ferent way. While Daddy was the one who got things done, Mom Unser was the glue that held things together. She was incredibly im-portant to all of us, and our success. She became my secretary when Daddy passed away.

First, Mom helped Daddy run his business. She did all the book-keeping and paperwork, and was always helping out. She was always there to support us in our racing careers, and making sure we had food in our stomachs and a nice home to sleep in.

Here's a story about what a truly great person Mom was. You have to understand that she had lost one of her oldest sons, Jerry (Jerry and Louis were twins). Jerry died in May of 1959, after he crashed during practice trials for the Indianapolis 500. That hurts any mother, and

Mom Unser was no exception. Four years later, when I had the opportunity to go to Indianapolis for the Indy 500, I had to break the news to her. After being told, she went into her and Daddy's bedroom, and closed the door. I could hear her crying. Fifteen minutes later, she came out with her bags packed and said, "Let's go." That's a special, special woman in my world.

Uncle Louis was my hero, even though he had caused so much trouble for us. Remember, he went back on his promise to let me drive his car down the mountain when I was 16, then he ratted on my brother Al for being underage (only by two months!) on the Hill Climb. Despite these issues, I still liked Uncle Louis, and he often helped me at Pikes Peak.

Then there were my brothers—Jerry, Louis, and Al. Jerry and Louis were older than me by 15 months. Jerry was a great driver, and it was a real heartbreak for our whole family when he died. Louis was an absolute wild-man as a driver, but was diagnosed with Multiple Sclerosis in 1962. Louis then focused on building engines, and became a famous raceboat engine builder in Anaheim, California. He built me a few really good racecar engines for Pikes Peak that I set records with.

The youngest of the four Unser boys was Al. There's a great photo of Mom, Daddy, me, Louis, and Al standing together at Indianapolis in 1965. Mom is dressed up nice, Daddy looks like he's ready to go to work, Louis's already got dirt and grease on his knees from crawling under my car, I'm wearing a sweaty driver's suit after a day of practice, and Al is standing there calm and clean in a nice plaid shirt, looking innocent as hell. Don't ever let that innocence fool you—under that cool look is one helluva competitor. Wow, what a driver Al was! In his day, he was the best!

We could tell Al had a lot of natural talent when he was still young. He and I won many races in the mid '50s before I went into the Air Force. After I left for the service, some of the other drivers started to play it pretty rough with Al. Daddy called me and told me what was happening. I made it back for the weekends, to help straighten things out with the other drivers. It wasn't just that the other drivers had to deal with me—they had to deal with two of us, and that was just too much for them to handle.

Just as I was there for Al, he was there for me. I had a horrible crash at Phoenix, Arizona in November, 1973. I was leading the race when Gary Bettenhausen pushed me into the wall coming out of turn two. I was knocked unconscious. I eventually saw the film, and it wasn't pretty. The fence and desert dirt exploded as if a bomb had struck. The car careened off the embankment, and continued to disintegrate as it spiraled down the track toward the infield. Spectators and track personnel ducked for cover as tires blew off and the metal parts flew everywhere like shrapnel. All that was left of the car was the capsule I was sitting in. The back of the seat had been ripped away, exposing my back, and the fuel spilled all over the racetrack, surrounding my car.

The yellow caution flag came out as sirens wailed and rescue teams scrambled to the accident. They weren't the best rescue team in the world, because not one of them was willing to walk through the pool of fuel to get me out. I guess they figured I was dead. Parnelli Jones was watching the race, and from where he was, he thought for sure I was dead. So, nobody was in a real hurry to pull me out of there, unless they were willing to be chalked up as fatalities themselves.

My brother Al was in the race, and slowed down under the caution. He didn't know who was involved in the accident—he just knew the yellow caution flag was out. As he came up to the accident scene, he saw the back of my uniform sticking out of what was left of my seat. I guess it was a blessing that the crash was so bad that the back of the seat had been ripped clean off, exposing my uniform. Otherwise, Al wouldn't have known it was me. Recognizing my jacket, he slowed down, pulled to the infield, and stopped, taking himself out of the race.

Al jumped out of his car and sprinted through the fuel-soaked track to pull my unconscious body out of the wreck. Then he stayed by my side the whole time they were working to revive me. He even boarded the MediVac Helicopter and accompanied me to the hospital. Al told me that when we got to the hospital, it was the typical emergency room scene: nobody really in a hurry to get anything done. He walked out into the hall and saw a doctor walking by. Al asked, "Do you fix broken bones?" The doctor, who happened to be an orthopedic surgeon, looked at Al and grinned, "Why, yes!" Al said, "Good! You're hired!" Al grabbed the doctor, dragged him into my room and had him start working on me.

Today, my best friend and business partner is my wife, Lisa. She helps me by managing the many business activities I'm involved with and runs the office we have in our home. Lisa has her pilot's license and is a good hunter, so there are many things we have in common and enjoy doing together. She's great with the racing family and all the businesses we are involved with. I'm really lucky to have someone who means so many good things to me.

I was fortunate to have such a good family to help me in my career. You may not have that kind of support, but that doesn't mean you can't have an adoptive family to help you succeed.

THE FAMILY OF RACE CAR DRIVERS

Racecar drivers are a different breed of cat, make no mistake about it. We know we're taking an incredible risk to feed our competitive desires and our thirst for the thrill that speed gives us. We may be really competitive, and at times totally dislike each other, but the simultaneous danger and ultimate thrill of speed bonds us in a rather unique way. We're an incredibly close family in that sense.

I don't know why I click with certain people right away, but it just happens. Roger McCluskey was one of those people. He became one of my best friends. Roger was such a good friend, he helped me fly my airplane even though he *hated* flying.

One time, Roger, Parnelli Jones, and I flew in my single-engine plane to three midget races in a row. The first race was at Ascot in Los Angeles followed the next day with one in Albuquerque, then the day after, a third race was in Tucson. After we raced in Los Angeles, we didn't head directly to Albuquerque. We decided to fly over to Las Vegas first. Following a sleepless night in Las Vegas, we headed for Albuquerque. I was the only one of the three who had a pilot's license, but Parnelli was a student pilot, so I let him fly. Well, after we were part way to Albuquerque, Parnelli and I pulled a little joke on Roger, letting one of the fuel tanks run empty. One of the engines sputtered and choked, and I started yelling at Parnelli telling him he had forgotten to fuel up. Roger was two or three shades of green by then, so I switched over to another fuel tank, and the engine sprang to life. Well, Parnelli and I had a good laugh at Roger's expense, but it was all in good racing driver humor.

I think what clicked between Roger McCluskey and me was we thought alike as drivers. He helped me learn how to drive in sprint car races—showing me how to work the high-banked tracks and what to watch out for. He educated me about the other drivers and their tendencies. He also showed me the best setups for my sprint car. That's why I didn't hesitate when Wayne Leary asked me to help set up Roger McCluskey to qualify for the Indy 500 in 1971. Like I said, what goes around comes around.

There are many other drivers I felt really close to, and still feel close to many of them today. The list includes Parnelli Jones, one of the greatest ever, who helped me get into the Indianapolis 500. A.J. Foyt used to help me with my sprint car setups. Johnny Rutherford was one of the best I ever ran against, and of course, my brother, Al Unser, Sr., who was a great driver on any kind of racing course. Don Branson was the best qualifier I ever saw. Don was about as good a friend as Roger McCluskey. It was a terrible heartache for me to see him killed at Ascot back in 1967. The reason the list is long is for a good reason. They are really good people, and people that I absolutely respect and admire.

OWNERS AND SPONSORS

The best owners and sponsors were the ones who got involved with the race teams. For many years, I had some really great owners and sponsors who ran good companies and treated me and the crew like family. Ozzie Olson of Olsonite, Earle Jorgensen of Jorgensen Steel, Bill Clayton of Clayton Industries, Gordon Van Liew of The Vita Fresh Orange Juice Company, Bob Wilke of Leader Cards, Dutch Sproul of Sproul Homes, Frank Arciero of Arciero Construction, and of course Dan

Gurney and Roger Penske were (and some still are) great owners of race teams and good businesspeople who ran gold-plated companies.

Ozzie Olson was a family type of owner. Not only was he a second-generation family business owner, but his people were all part of the family. He got close to them, just as he got close to his customers, and his race team. Ozzie would go out with us and just have a great time, not because he was playing the corporate game, but because he genuinely liked what he did and who he did it with. He had fun running a business, and we had fun working with him.

Bill Clayton of Clayton Industries was a sponsor for three years from 1972 to 1974. After a race, he always invited his customers to a hospitality tent. Clayton Industries made dynamometers used to test race engines and automotive emissions. Besides selling dynamometers to race teams, their big customers were in the emissions testing market—the "Big Three" auto makers and the EPA. Our races in Indianapolis and Milwaukee had a pretty big turnout in the after-race hospitality tent. I always made sure that I went there after getting cleaned up to meet Clayton's customers and thank them for attending. It was a good thing to do, and I liked seeing Bill Clayton get involved with his customers. I learned a lot by watching those interactions.

Not all sponsors or car owners were as involved as those people were. One year we had a deal with Arco, but it was a dead relationship. They gave us money, but there was no activity behind the money: they just threw money at us and said win. That's not the familial relationship I like to have with a sponsor. It doesn't work only with their blood—it has to include their sweat and tears in order to work right. There has to be some effort to do something that goes with the money. Money helps, but effort gets things done better. Money and effort together get a *lot* of things done a whole lot faster.

In Chapter 6, Races Are Won in the Pits, I pointed out how I needed sponsors to help fund my growth. If you can get close to a sponsor, or in your case, perhaps a bank or investor, you're one step ahead in the game. Of course, you can only get close—become family—if they let you in. Once you're in their family, cherish the privilege, because that's exactly what it is—a privilege. You can also develop a real good network of business contacts when the money people invite you into their family.

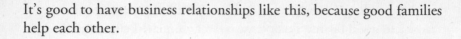

It's good to have business relationships like this, because good families help each other.

THE ADMINISTRATIVE FAMILY

On a race team, the crew takes care of all the details so the driver can focus on racing. The importance of good crew was discussed in detail in Chapter 6, Races Are Won in the Pits. One thing worthy of mentioning is the fact that the crew and I had to become family. We had to bond in order to understand the subtleties of our personalities. Tension could get high and tempers flare when winning was on the line. Knowing one another's personalities became vital if we were to have any degree of success. John Miller was one of the best engine builders ever, but a real quiet person. And we accepted that. Just as a family may have a quiet kid and a wild kid, racing crews (and business teams in general) will most certainly have individuals with varying personalities. What separates teams that become families from those that don't is the degree of respect they share for one another's differences.

When a family is running on all cylinders, it attracts good people. Ace Hartline was one of those people. He owned the Butler Paper Company in Phoenix, Arizona. He was well-heeled and a great businessman. Ace was a helper on my pit crews, and he followed me from team to team for many years. He always had a clean helmet ready to go for me at every race, and it was somewhat of a ceremony when Ace handed it to me. I also remember there always being a clean rag in one of Ace's pockets, and his making sure all the little things were done. They may have been little things, but they needed to be done and Ace did them well.

In business, you need the details to be taken care of, just like the race crew. An absolutely invaluable person is an administrative assistant. A good administrative assistant is like getting an entire pit crew and mechanic rolled up into one person. I don't know where I would be without the great administrative assistants I've had over my long career. In the early days, Mom did most of it. She took care of all the details, and all the things that I personally didn't have time for, but that needed to be done. In the '70s and '80s, my then wife, Marsha, was absolutely invaluable in this regard. Today, my wife, Lisa not only handles most of the details, but she does a lot of the business planning and makes sure all our computers are running properly. We are good business partners. She also does much of the flying of our planes we use on our business trips.

Bruce Barnes, my agent, had a great administrative assistant—Liz Dibblee. She had to help with 15 of the athletes Bruce represented. In the sports contract and celebrity appearance world, everything is a last-minute rush job. This includes promotions, events, speaking engagements, and the numerous endorsement proposals and contracts that are continuously changed. Liz handled it all with class and confidence, and didn't let the panic situations sway her from doing a good job. She was definitely a member of Bruce's business family.

THE EXTENDED UNSER RACING FAMILY

While my family was a great asset in my career, there were other people who became family. Even when we were kids growing up, we had another set of parents other than Daddy and Mom raising us. While Mom was helping Daddy run his downtown car repair garages, Bud Stagner and his wife ran the garage next to our house on Highway 66. Since they were around during the day, they were like daycare parents to us. They helped raise the Unser clan while Daddy and Mom were working.

Many years later, I was a daycare "father" to my good friend Howard Millican's son, Ronnie Dawes. While I liked Howard, and Howard was a member of the extended racing family, he wasn't such a good father all the time. He had a drinking problem, and bingeing as much as Howard did was not something a father should be doing. His wife divorced him and remarried a real nice guy, whose last name was Dawes. He adopted Ronnie, hence the last name Dawes.

Ronnie came by my shop one day when he was about 17 years old looking for work. I gave him something to do, and, man, I'm telling you, he learned quick. I realized in a hurry that Ronnie had a lot of talent, and I could help him out. He was a good kid, and deserved a good chance. So, I offered him a full-time job and took him under my wing, making him a part of the family.

Well, one good thing led to another, and pretty soon Ronnie was the chief mechanic for my son Bobby Jr.'s race team. Ronnie continued to develop as a great mechanic, and became well-known in the racing circuit. Eventually, he became the youngest chief mechanic ever to win the Indy 500 when he was the chief mechanic for Buddy Lazier's car in the 1996 race. I was really proud of what he accomplished.

Even my house was a part of the racing family. Built on old Route 66, I usually left the front part of it unlocked so that drivers passing through could "crash" for a while if necessary. I slept in another area toward the back, and usually would never hear them if they came in late. Racing teams knew about "hotel Unser," where they had access to a pull-out couch, bar, pool table, and Jacuzzi. They would stop by in the middle of the night on their way to a race and sleep for a few hours. Sometimes I'd get up in the morning not knowing if someone had been there. Later that day I'd be at a race in California, and someone would walk up to me and say, "Bobby! Thanks for letting me stay at your place last night!"

Here's an example about the racing family, and how tightly it's bonded. Twenty years after I retired from racing, in the summer of 2001, I went to the Goodwood Festival of Speed in England with my wife, Lisa. I was invited to drive the Penske car we won the Indy 500 with in 1981. This wasn't a real race, just a demo of running the car around a road course in England for show-and-tell. It was a long flight from Albuquerque to London. Then there was a 90-minute drive from London out to the Penske shop in England. Arriving dead-ass tired from the long trip, what I saw stunned me. There was my 1981 Team Penske Indy race car, ready to go as though I was going to race the Indy 500 that day.

Three mechanics and a fabricator were standing next to the car, ready to go over the setups. The car had an entirely new suspension and a fresh engine. I'll bet the suspension alone cost Roger a good $150,000 to build, but there are no shortcuts with him when it comes to doing anything. He puts value in his racing family, and that's one of the ways he succeeds.

Even the car setup sheet, with all the settings for the chassis was there, filled out just the way I would have it for race day. Nick Goosey, the person who built Penske's cars, was there. Looking at that car sitting there waiting for me with a super crew was just like the scene in the Danny Kaye and Bing Crosby classic movie *White Christmas* when all the troops were lined up waiting for their General to inspect them. It brought tears to my eyes, because it said everything about how close the racing family is—how we don't forget about each other and our bond is to the end. More businesses would be much better off today if they treated their employees like family. There certainly would be more confidence and trust in corporate executives.

FANS

Racing is like any other business: with no *fans*, there's no race. With no *customers*, there's no business. The more customers you have, the better product you can produce. More satisfied customers bring more revenues, and with more revenues you can make better products. With better products, you get more satisfied customers. They feed each other.

You can't build a successful business without catering to your customers. If there is a number one priority in business, it is the customer. Look at any successful business model today, and you'll see the main driving force behind what it does is focus on the customer. The number one component to building a good team is to get the customers on the team by giving them what they want—a good show. Today, no one seems to be doing that better than NASCAR, although the Indy Racing League has had some of the best racing lately. And with Chris Pook in charge of CART, look for some exciting changes to take place in open-wheel racing real soon.

Coming from a poor background helped me respect the fans. I knew they had worked hard all week. Then they took their hard-earned money and came to see the race on the weekend. Racing was their choice for entertainment, for fun, for blowing off some steam. They brought their friends, their dates, and their families. It was a big event for them. They deserved a good show, and I always did my best to give it to them.

Many athletes have a hard time with this. They have a passion for their sport, but they often shut the fans out. They're not comfortable in the public environment. I understand that—I hated it when my high school English teacher paraded me in front of class to tell everyone how well I did winning the races the weekend before. That was one of the main reasons I quit high school. I was just fifteen years-old, and really embarrassed. Eventually, I got over the notoriety issue—I had to, otherwise I would have had some serious problems. Athletes have to learn to deal with the fact that their competitive spirit and high level of performance has thrust them into the spotlight.

Some business leaders today isolate themselves from their customers. This is a horrible practice. How can they make good decisions if they don't understand who their customers are or what their customers want? Customers make up the largest part of the business "family"— they are the ones who hold you in judgment on how good your products and services perform.

I get about as many autograph requests in the mail today as I did when I was driving. I love them, and reply to every one of them. Every one gets a personalized, signed autograph. Why not? They've taken the time to send a personal note to me, so I can take the time to respond and help make their day. It makes everyone feel better.

Once back in the '70s at the Rex Mays Classic in Milwaukee, I was signing autographs. A boy came up to me and asked me for my autograph. I smiled, talked to him a little, and gave him my autograph. Several years later, I was sitting in the New York office of Dennis Swanson, the President of ABC Sports. He was one *big* man. This was the first time we had met. We were discussing my upcoming move from NBC to become ABC's racing sports analyst. Then he told me a story about how he watched a famous racecar driver sign an autograph for a fan at the Rex Mays Classic in Milwaukee a few years earlier. Dennis saw how elated the fan was, because this was his favorite racecar driver. It turns out that the fan was his son, and the driver was me. The job at ABC was almost mine before I walked in the door. As I said before, it pays to do good things for the right reasons—you never know who's watching.

Albuquerque, New Mexico

. . . *"So I finally get the hang of this—I can drive through these red lights and don't have a worry in the world because I have my Albuquerque police pass, Mr. Bobby Unser. Talk about pull.*

"I drove through seven consecutive red lights. Then I came upon a green light, and as I was about to go through it Bobby yelled, 'Stop!'

"So I slammed on the brakes. 'What the hell was that for, Bobby?!'

"Then he said, 'Al might be coming the other way!' "

≡ PIT STOP POINTERS

- Surround yourself with a tight-knit group of career "family" members.
- Develop a peer network.
- Include financial benefactors in the family.
- Become family with your "crew members"—the detailers and administrators.
- Treat customers like family.

CONCLUSION

If any one word or thought sums up both my racing and business career, it's this: Desire! That's the one secret great equalizer in every person's career. Not education. Not being born with hidden talents. Desire. Nothing fuels success like desire.

Whatever you elect to do in your life or career, let your passion dictate where you make your turns. Let the fuel of desire drive you through the tough times, and propel you upward during the good times. You'll discover that your belief in what you do is more important than any of the obstacles thrown in your path. The taste of victory will then endure forever.

Go fast, lead, win. That's what life's about. Waiting for someone else to do something or some other event to occur won't get you anywhere. You've got places to go and things to do, and you can't do them waiting for others. So, get going, and go fast—you'll learn quicker, and stand out more. You never know who's watching. Then, figure out how to lead. Not by announcing it with your mouth, by doing it with your actions. Leading races wasn't something I talked about, it was something I did. Eventually, after leading enough, you'll win. Go fast, lead, win.

As much as I believe in motivation and taking initiative, I'm not really an optimist. I'm a *believer*! There's a huge difference: Optimists live in some dream world where every day is sunny. Believers hold the sunshine in their souls, but accept the fact the weather outside can be downright lousy at times. When the passion is so deep inside you that you're able to overcome all challenges, you have won the toughest part of any race—you've qualified. Now all you have to do is plan, drive smart, and finish strong.

If you do what's in your soul, success will come. Guaranteed. And in the end, you'll realize it wasn't the financial reward that drove you there, it was a deep burning feeling. It was desire.

AFTERWORD

Recently, society has been rocked by questionable leadership in business, in churches, and in our governments. Egotistical maniacs, greed-driven desires, and hidden personal agendas have all but ruined the public's view of successful individuals. Worse still, anyone of character with leadership capability averts the glare of the spotlight, knowing that as soon as they ascend the throne, they become a target for career assassins lurking in the shadows. And, if by some miracle, they reach the top alive, they seem to be subject to the ever-present legions of back-stabbing Brutus', the ultimate betrayers of trust.

I never met Bobby Unser before my involvement with this book. Initially, I thought he would tell me a few stories, and that would be that.

Then I met Bobby Unser. He walks into a room like a cowboy—tall, confident, and in command. His feet are on the ground. There's no snobbish arrogance, notwithstanding the countless trophies, plaques and press clippings adorning the walls of his ranch house in Albuquerque. Finally, the bonus: He has a passion and focus not only to get things done right, but to do so in a brutally honest way.

When he talked about business, I realized this was not an ordinary athlete talking to me. This was a man with deep, sound principles. If more leaders were as tall as Bobby is in his convictions, yet as grounded as he is in his human nature, we'd all be better for it. There's no bullshit with Bobby Unser. He tells it straight—like it or hate it—you know where he's coming from.

Bobby's ex-wife, Marsha once said that Bobby had a "built-in switch, where he can turn things on and off in a moment." I would only alter her quote in this sense: Bobby has a built-in switch, and he can change from total focus on one subject to another in a flash, but this switch does *not* have an "off" position. There is no "off" position with Bobby Unser. He is always "on"—he just changes the channel.

What I think is the most impressive aspect of Bobby's thinking is his ability to simultaneously focus on a detail and see the big picture. He focuses hard "100 yards down the race track" on whatever is immediately in front of him, but also has great peripheral vision to know what is going on around him. Then he uses all this information, compares it to his prethought strategy, and quickly adapts to the situation.

Bobby and Bruce Barnes sent me a list of executives and celebrities to contact for the book. Not only was the list impressive—Roger Penske, Parnelli Jones, Dan Gurney, Dennis Swanson, Kevin Wulff, Brian Williams, Dennis Lewin, Doug Sellars, to name a few—but everyone was willing to talk about Bobby Unser. The one common theme throughout these conversations about Bobby was that he impressed people with his desire, his passion, his energy, and his commitment to get things done.

For the privilege of sharing the last few months with a winner like Bobby Unser, I am truly grateful.

Paul Pease, 2002

BOBBY UNSER
3 Time Indy 500 Winner

BIRTHDATE: February 20, 1934
RESIDENCE: Albuquerque, New Mexico
BIRTHPLACE: Colorado Springs, Colorado
CHILDREN: Bobby Jr., Cindy, Robby, and Jeri
HOBBIES: Hunting, flying, snowmobiling, and motorcycling

Racing Highlights

- 3-time Indy 500 Champion—1968, 1975, and 1981
- 2-time National Champion—1968 and 1974
- 35 Career Indy Car Victories (4th All-time)
- 2-time series winner of the International Race of Champions
- 49 Career Pole Positions (3rd All-time)
- Indy 500 Hall of Fame Member
- Inducted into the International Motorsports Hall of Fame
- 13-time winner Pikes Peak Hill Climb and inducted into the Pikes Peak Hill Climb Hall of Fame
- 8 "500" Mile Victories (Indy 500, 3; California 500, 4; Pocono 500, 1)

- 1989—Inducted into AARWBA's Legends in Racing.
- 1993—Won inaugural Jaguar/Fast Masters Racing Series
- 1993—Bonneville Salt Flats—set new land speed record: 223.709 mph

Business Affiliations

- ABC Sports Television
- A.D.T. Automotive, Inc.
- Audi of America
- BASF Corporation
- Bombardier Corporation
- Canadian Broadcasting Corporation Television
- Chrysler Corporation
- General Motors/Chevrolet/Cadillac/Pontiac/Oldsmobile
- IBM
- K-Tel, Incorporated
- Mechanical Industries
- Mid-Western Transit
- Mobil Oil Corporation
- Holiday Rambler Corporation
- Torco International Corporation
- Williams Group International

Project Achievements

- Development work and test driver for the General Motors front-wheel drive development project (Toronado)
- High performance testing work for the Chevrolet Division of General Motors
- Racecar and passenger car development, and racecar driver for Audi of America
- Considered by racing and automotive engineers as the most qualified chassis expert in America

- Vast experience and knowledge in racing and high performance passenger car engines
- Currently expert witness specializing in accident reconstruction analysis for automotive, truck, and school bus litigation

Career Update

Three-time Indy 500 winner, Bobby Unser, will be busier than ever this year given his vast involvement with corporations and numerous public speaking engagements and appearances.

Bobby returned behind the wheel in 1998 for the 76th annual Pikes Peak International Hill Climb by competing in the inaugural "Challenge of Champions" race. Since 1990, Bobby has commentated for CART Indy Car races in Toronto and Vancouver, Canada. He will continue his promotional and advertising appearances for several of the major companies involved in auto racing or accident reconstruction.

Acting as an advisor during his son Robby's rookie run at the 1998 Indy 500 (Robby placed 5th), Bobby has also aided Robby with his victories at Pikes Peak (1987–1990, 1992, 1995–1996) and with his win in the championship in the American Indy Car Series (1987).

Race Analyst and Commentator for CBC Television (1998–1999):
- Molson Indy Toronto Race—Ontario, Canada
- Molson Indy Vancouver Race—British Columbia, Canada

Automobile Racing Commentator for ABC Television (1987–1997):
- Indianapolis 500 Qualifying
- Indianapolis 500 Race
- PPG Indy Car Races
- IROC Races

Other Projects:
- Worked with Anlon Press to produce a book titled *Unser, An American Family Portrait*.
- Appears as a guest speaker at an average of 40 functions all over the country during the year.

Career Highlights

1949   Started racing stock cars in New Mexico.

1950   Captured Southwest Modified Stock Car Championship at age 16.

1951   Recaptured Southwest Modified Stock Car title.

1952   Moved into midget and sprint car ranks. Wasted little time finding the winner's circle with 3 wins.

1953–55 United States Air Force.

1956   Won Championship car division at the Pikes Peak Hill Climb. Started incredible record of 13 "Hill" titles. Only driver in history to win all 3 divisions: Open wheel racing, stock cars, and sports cars.

1963   Ran first Indy 500, but an early accident forced him out of the event.

1964   Ran Championship cars as well as sprint cars.

1965   Finished 7th in final USAC Championship points.

1966   Placed 6th in final USAC Championship points.

1967   Won first Indy car race at Mosport, Ontario, Canada. Not known as a "road racer" at the time, but set a new track record. Finished 3rd in USAC points.

1968   Won first Indy 500 at record speed. Captured the USAC national title. Became first driver to run over 170 mph at Indianapolis. Also won events at Las Vegas, Phoenix, and Trenton; first of 6 Trenton wins.

1969   Finished 3rd in USAC standings. Won Langhorne, PA, race.

1970   Placed 2nd to brother, Al, in final USAC standings. Won Langhorne, PA, event for 2nd straight year.

1971   Won Milwaukee and Trenton races. Finished 6th in USAC point standings.

1972   Set new qualifying mark at Indianapolis at 195.940 mph. Was fastest qualifier in eight of nine races. Led all nine races for total of 520 laps. Became first driver to ever qualify with an average speed over 200 mph (201.374). Won Phoenix twice, Trenton and Milwaukee races.

1973   Qualified 2nd at Indy 500, led for 39 laps before engine failure. Won Milwaukee race.

1974   Won 2nd USAC National Championship. Won races at Ontario, Michigan, and Trenton twice. Placed 2nd at Indy. Named Martini & Rossi "Driver of the Year."

1975   Won his second Indy 500 in Dan Gurney's Eagle. Finished 3rd in USAC standings. Won prestigious International Race of Champions (IROC) title.

1976   Won his second California 500 at Ontario, as well as the Phoenix event. Notched 6th in USAC standings.

1979   Won six races on the newly-formed CART series, including a third California 500, Trenton twice, Michigan twice and Watkins Glen. Placed 2nd in final standings.

1980   Won four events, including fourth California 500, Pocono 500, Milwaukee and Watkins Glen. Again finished 2nd in final CART points.

1981   Captured 3rd Indy 500. Placed 7th in CART standings.

1983   Won Pikes Peak Hill Climb as car owner/team manager-driver, Al Unser, Jr.

1986   Won Pikes Peak Hill Climb as driver in the Audi Sport Quattro SL. Entered by the Audi factory.

1993   Won inaugural Jaguar/Fast Master Championship at Indianapolis Raceway Park in August. Bobby also set a new land speed record of 223.709 mph at the Bonneville Salt Flats in the "D" class with a gas-powered modified roadster in September.

1994   Was inducted into the Novi Motorsports Hall of Fame.

1998–
Present   Bobby continues his involvement with corporate speaking engagements, product endorsements and personal appearances, as well as accident reconstruction analysis for automotive, truck, and school bus litigation.

Totals

35 Career Indy Car Wins

2 USAC National Championships (1968 and 1974)

3 Indy 500 wins (1968, 1975 and 1981)

4 California 500 wins (1974, 1976, 1979, and 1980)

1 Pocono 500 win (1980)

13 Pikes Peak Hill Climb Championships

INDEX